W. Laird Clowes

Black America

a study of the ex-slave and his late master

W. Laird Clowes

Black America
a study of the ex-slave and his late master

ISBN/EAN: 9783744737937

Printed in Europe, USA, Canada, Australia, Japan

Cover: Foto ©ninafisch / pixelio.de

More available books at **www.hansebooks.com**

BLACK AMERICA:

A STUDY OF THE EX-SLAVE AND HIS LATE MASTER.

BY

W. LAIRD CLOWES

REPRINTED, WITH LARGE ADDITIONS, FROM "THE TIMES."

CASSELL & COMPANY, LIMITED:

LONDON, PARIS & MELBOURNE.

1891.

CONTENTS.

INTRODUCTION.

In the autumn of 1890 I was commissioned by *The Times* to go to the southern part of the United States in order to study upon the spot the conditions of the very extraordinary social problem which has gradually arisen there during the past two hundred years, and which has assumed new and peculiar importance since the manumission of the negroes and "coloured" people, and the nominal extension to them of all the privileges of American citizenship. For this study I was in some degree prepared, not only by a long-indulged fondness for the subject, but also by a previous residence in the United States. The result of my inquiries took the form of a series of ten letters, which appeared in *The Times* in November and December, 1890, and in January of the present year. These letters, with considerable additions, and with such corrections as fuller knowledge and the kind assistance of numerous correspondents have suggested, are now reprinted. They embrace, I think, a fair and comprehensive view of the problem in all its most significant aspects. I have conversed, without prejudice, with whites and with blacks, with Republicans and with Democrats, with men who are in office, and with men who are anxious to find themselves there; and I have not consciously closed my ears to any argument from any quarter. This volume, therefore, may, I trust, be accepted as containing a true account of a state of affairs which is without parallel in the history of modern civilisation, and which is, no doubt, destined to exercise a momentous, and possibly a terrible, influence upon the future of America.

Briefly summarised, the situation in the South is as follows. The inhabitants, black and white, have all been given equal rights by the amended Constitution of the Union. Each man of full age is as much a citizen as his fellow. That is the

view of the law, from Maine to California. But
in the South there are several millions of people
whose veins contain more or less negro blood.
A generation ago these people, or their parents,
were, almost without exception, slaves in the
hands of the Southern whites. A great revolution was effected. The black suddenly ceased to
be a slave; and, within a few years, he was presented not only with his freedom, but also, in
theory at least, with all the privileges that were
previously the sole possession of the white. This
raising of the black from the depths of slavery to
the heights of citizenship was the work of outside
forces. It was not done by the Southern white,
nor, save as regards mere manumission, was it
done with his approval or consent. He was not
in a position to resist the will of the victorious
North. Indeed, the North imperiously forced its
will upon him, and even used as its agents the
very blacks who had but just been liberated from
bondage. This policy created bad blood between
whites and blacks. From the moment of its full
enforcement harmonious working between blacks

and whites in the field of politics, and in most other spheres, became impossible. The Southern white assumed a sullenly rebellious attitude. He determined that he would render a dead letter the grant of citizenship to the black; and to a very large extent he has done so. But, in the meantime, the black, in certain districts, has been increasing more rapidly than the white; and to-day, in some of those districts, he actually outnumbers him, while in others he equals him, and will outnumber him in the early future. Still, nevertheless—even where he is in a conclusive minority—the Southern white persists in his dogged resolution not to allow the black to meddle with the machinery of government, not to permit him for an instant to wear the full robe of citizenship that has been presented to him by the North. This is the bare kernel of the situation. Hitherto the black has, upon the whole, meekly submitted to this illegal deprivation of his rights. Can he be expected to submit for ever? Or will he some day attempt by force to seize that to which he is by law entitled? Should he ever do this, either alone or backed by all the resources of the North, there will be a scene of horror such as the South never witnessed in the darkest days of the Civil War. So much is absolutely certain.

What follows aspires to be an impartial review not only of the present aspects but also of the past history of the complex problem which has thus been created. It includes, also, a humble suggestion for the permanent solution of that problem. I have attempted to show, firstly, where the problem exists in its most pressing and dangerous form; secondly, the reasons which impel the South to refuse to constitutionally solve the problem by allowing the majority to rule; thirdly, the intolerable position of the Southern black; and, fourthly, the intolerable position of the Southern white. The position of all parties concerned naturally demands that some way out of the difficulty should be invented. I have, therefore, gone on to show, fifthly, what solutions have been advocated, and why they must all be ineffective; and, sixthly, what appears to me to

be the best, the most just, and the only radical
solution.

This solution is one which, I admit, I almost
despair of seeing carried out. The peaceable
removal of the negroes from the United States,
and their establishment across the ocean in a
country and in circumstances that would be
propitious not only to their own development
but also to the development of their barbarous
kindred, are measures which would involve very
great expense. But it is not, I believe, on the
score of expense that the average American is
likely to reject the scheme. His great inherit-
ance provides him with wealth more than sufficient to enable him to pay all his debts, including
those huge ones which he owes to the black.
He is much more likely to adopt a characteristic
attitude such as he has adopted in the past
towards many other threatening questions. One
of the most distinguished of living American
statesmen said to me in November last: " If my
country should ever come to frightful disaster,
it will be, I am convinced, because it is the

incurable habit of my countrymen to cherish the belief that they are so much the special care of Providence that it would be superfluous, on their part, to take even simple and ordinary precautions for their own protection."

.

BLACK AMERICA.

CHAPTER I.

THE BLACK BELT.

THE total population of the United States, exclusive of Alaska and of the Indian Territory, was, according to the official returns of the Tenth Census, 50,155,783. This Census was taken as long ago as 1880; but it is, and will for some time continue to be, the latest enumeration concerning which full statistical details are in possession of the world. An Eleventh Census was taken in June, 1890. This, so far as has as yet been ascertained, fixes the population of the great Republic at 62,622,250.* The details of it are, however, still unknown. We are altogether in the dark as to how many of the people are males and how many females, how many white and how many coloured; and months, if not years, may be expected to elapse before the hard-working Census Bureau at Washington shall find itself in a position to enlighten us upon these and other particular points of interest. But there is no reason

* NOTE.—See Appendix.

B

to suppose that the full details of the Eleventh
Census will, when they are published, greatly
surprise the statistical experts who have made a
special study of the increase of American population in the past and of its probable increase in
the future; nor are there any signs that the results of the Eleventh Census will, upon one point of
special significance, be much more reassuring than
were those of the Tenth. That point of special
significance is the rate of increase of the coloured
people in certain extensive sections of the old
slave-holding States of the South. This rate of
increase has hitherto been vastly superior to that
of the white people in the same districts, and is
a thing of no new growth. The four States,
Virginia, North Carolina, South Carolina, and
Georgia, were numbered for the first time in
1790. Their white and coloured populations in
that year and in the year 1880, and the rates of
increase per cent. during the ninety intermediate
years, are shown in the following tables :—

WHITE POPULATION.

	1790.	1880.	Increase per Cent.
Virginia	442,117	880,858	99·2
North Carolina	288,204	867,242	200·9
South Carolina	140,178	391,105	179·0
Georgia ..	52,886	816,906	1,442·9

COLOURED POPULATION.

	1790.	1880.	Increase per Cent.
Virginia	305,493	631,616	106·7
North Carolina	105,547	531,277	402·4
South Carolina	108,895	604,332	454·9
Georgia	29,662	725,133	2,344·6

While, therefore, in the ninety years the white population of the four States has grown from 923,385 to only 2,956,111, the coloured population has grown from 549,597 to 2,492,358. In other words, while the whites have increased only 220·1 per cent., the blacks have increased 353·4 per cent., and the latter have been continuing to increase with superior speed in face of the facts that now for more than a generation black immigration has practically ceased, and that the black race is considerably shorter-lived than the white. It is remarkable, too, that in each of the four States the rate of increase has been greater among the blacks than among the whites.

In only the above-mentioned four of the eight old Slave States of the South was there a Census in 1790. The first census of Mississippi was taken in 1800, of Louisiana in 1810, of Alabama in 1820, and of Florida in 1830. The first enumerations of the eight States showed a total white population of 1,066,711 ; the Census of

1880 showed the white population to be 4,695,253,
an increase of 340·2 per cent. On the other
hand, the first enumerations of the eight States
showed a coloured population of but 654,308,
while the Census of 1880 showed a coloured
population of no less than 4,353,097, or an
increase of 563·7 per cent. Whereas, therefore, at
the earliest enumerations the blacks formed only
about 38 per cent. of the population, they formed
in 1880 about 48 per cent. In short, in these
States, and in the period under review, the blacks
steadily drew ever nearer and nearer to the attainment of a numerical majority. In 1860 they
were still nearly half a million behind the whites.
To-day, in the eight old Slave States of the South
the whites and the blacks are practically equal
in numbers, and in several individual States the
blacks have a formidable and growing majority.

It is in these last States most particularly
that what is known as the Negro Problem constitutes the most serious and complex social
question of the hour. For most of the other
States of the Union the problem possesses as yet
only a secondary interest. The total number of
negroes and coloured people in the whole of the
United States in 1880 was 6,580,793. Of these,
4,353,097 lived, as has been seen, in the eight
old Slave States of the South, and there formed

practically one-half of the population; 1,660,674
lived in the seven border States, Delaware, Maryland, Kentucky, Missouri, Arkansas, Texas, and
Tennessee, with 7,132,457 white fellow-citizens
around them; and the remaining 567,022 were
all but lost among the 31,575,260 whites—not to
mention the Chinese and Indians—in the rest of
the Union. So sparse, indeed, is the negro
population, save in the fifteen States that have
been named, that it need not be considered as a
factor of any weight whatever; but in those
fifteen States it is an ever-present force that
demands recognition by all political parties. The
fifteen States may be thus grouped :—

		Population, 1880.		Percentage of Coloured.
		White.	Coloured.	
A	Missouri ..	2,022,826	145,350	6·7
	Kentucky	1,377,179	271,451	16·4
	Delaware	120,160	26,442	18·1
	Maryland	724,693	210,230	22·4
	Texas ..	1,197,237	393,384	24·7
	Tennessee	1,138,831	403,151	26·1
	Arkansas	591,531	210,666	26·2
B	North Carolina	867,242	531,277	37·9
	Virginia ..	880,858	631,616	41·7
	Georgia ..	816,906	725,133	47·0
	Florida ..	142,605	126,690	47·1
	Alabama..	662,185	600,103	47·5
C	Louisiana	454,954	483,655	51·4
	Mississippi	479,398	650,291	57·5
	South Carolina..	391,105	604,332	60·6

In the States grouped under A, or, at least, in portions of them, the negro question occasionally assumes importance, though it is normally dormant. That it is not more often to the fore appears to result mainly from the political apathy or stupidity of the coloured population, which is frequently in a position, acting with organisation and method, to affect the balance of parties. In the States grouped under B the power of the negro is, theoretically, considerably greater. He has a vote in North Carolina if he be an actual citizen and not a convict; in Virginia if he be an actual citizen and not a lunatic, idiot, convict, duellist, or soldier; in Georgia if he be an actual taxpaying citizen and not a lunatic, idiot, or criminal; in Florida if he be a United States citizen, or have declared an intention of becoming one, and if he be not a lunatic, idiot, criminal, duellist, or bettor on elections; and in Alabama if he be a citizen, or have declared an intention of becoming one, and if he be not an idiot, an Indian, or a person convicted of crime. In none of these States is it definitely required that the negro voter shall be able to read or write; in only one is it required that he shall be even a taxpayer. The general requisites are merely manhood, a certain length of residence, and registration. Finally, in the States grouped under C, the negro is, if only he cared, and were permitted, to exercise his franchise, all-powerful. In Lousiana the qualification for the suffrage at present excludes no male citizen who, being of age, is not an idiot, lunatic, or criminal. In Mississippi the law is equally generous. In South Carolina the male citizen who is of age may vote unless he be a lunatic, an inmate of an asylum, almshouse, or prison, a duellist, or a soldier. There is no property or taxpaying quali-fication. The fifteenth amendment to the Con-stitution of the United States declares that "the right of the citizens of the United States to vote shall not be denied or abridged by the United States or any State on account of race, colour, or previous condition of servitude;" and the spirit of that amendment is, in theory, most fully honoured by all the Commonwealths. So completely is this the case that in 1880 the voting populations of the three States (C) were officially returned as:—

	White.	Coloured.
Louisiana	108,810	107,977
Mississippi	108,254	130,278
South Carolina	86,900	118,889

The slight coloured voting inferiority in Louisiana in 1880 is attributable to the high rate of infant and child mortality among the negroes as compared with the whites. It probably exists no longer. There is now, almost beyond question, a very considerable coloured voting majority in all these States, and probably a slight one in Alabama as well. The American Constitution recognises the right of the majority to rule. The impartial observer, therefore, might expect to find the government of Louisiana, Mississippi, and South Carolina, and possibly also of Alabama, almost, if not entirely, in the hands of the negro and coloured majority ; but upon his arrival in the South he finds no trace of anything of the kind. He finds, on the contrary, that the white man rules as supremely as he did in the days of slavery. The black man is permitted to have little or nothing to say upon the point; he is simply thrust on one side. At every political crisis the cry of the minority is, " This is a white man's question," and the cry is generally uttered in such a tone as to effectually warn off the black man from meddling with the matter.

I purpose later to show by what methods the white man attains his object when the usual cry fails to produce the whole of the expected result. I purpose also to show some of the reasons that are advanced by the Southern white man for his consistent refusal to countenance any negro interference in the affairs of State. For the present I confine myself to indicating the situation as it is and as it will be, and to suggesting that the existing white supremacy, whether it be for good or for evil, cannot continue indefinitely, and must eventually give place, either by free concession or as a tribute to brute force, to a new order of things.

Not only in Louisiana, Mississippi, and South Carolina, as wholes, is there a negro majority among the population, a similar majority exists in nearly all the low-lying portions of the Southern States, from the Chesapeake to Florida and from Florida to the borders of Mexico, and especially in those low-lying districts that are removed from the great towns.* The face of the country consists, speaking broadly, of hill-tracts, and of cities, where the whites are in a majority, and of lowlands, where the blacks are numerically supreme; and there are obvious natural reasons at the bottom of this division of the races. Heat is irksome to the Anglo-Saxon and correspondingly grateful to the negro. Trade, mining, and manufactures attract the white man; agriculture and tillage are preferred by the black. In the undrained lowlands the negro constitution defies fevers and other ills that often weaken if they

* NOTE.—See Map.

do not actually prove fatal to the white man's health. And so, apart from questions of births and deaths, some parts of the Southern States tend to every year become blacker, while others as steadily become whiter.

And the process which is initiated by geographical and climatic considerations is regularly aided by economical ones. The white man cannot compete as a labourer, or even as an artisan, upon equal terms with the black. He needs higher pay and better food. In black centres, therefore, the poor white man finds himself daily becoming more and more out of his element. Ordinary petty village trades, such as cobbling, tailoring, smithery, and carpentry, are thus, throughout the South, falling very much into the hands of the negroes; while the poor white men, who once had a monopoly of such humble pursuits, are going elsewhere in search of employment. They go, not to the uplands and cities of the South, but to the North, and, above all, to the new West, where every working man with strong arms, a good head, and an honest heart, has to-day the most brilliant of prospects.

The blacks, on the other hand, move about very little. They appreciate such little comforts as they have been able to gather around them

since their manumission, and neither the cold
North nor the half-settled West has any charms
for them. They have at present no strong
ambitions and very few wants. In the estimation of ninety-nine out of a hundred of them
a cabin in sunny South Carolina is a much more
desirable thing than a five-storeyed house in New
York or Chicago, and immeasurably preferable
to a store in Nebraska or a hut in Wyoming.
Moreover, the black likes to be among his black
kinsmen. A white man may occasionally persuade
himself to regard a negro as his brother, in
theory at least. The black man cares little for
theory, and bluntly recognises the white man as
a person of alien and, upon the whole, objectionable character from surface to core. And even
the most sympathetic white man prefers, in
practice, to be surrounded by a white majority
rather than by a black, especially when he is at
home in the bosom of his family.

These considerations, almost as much as the
superior fecundity and fewer wants of the negro,
are leading the Black Belt of the South to become
blacker than ever. White immigration has almost
ceased; white emigration is growing. In 1880,
as has been shown, there were 391,105 whites and
604,332 blacks in South Carolina. Of these only
7,686, or ·7 per cent., were of foreign birth.

Twenty years before, the number of foreign-born
people in the State had been 9,986, and in 1870
it had been 8,074. In the eight old Slave States
of the South (B and C) there were, in 1860,
148,662 foreign-born residents, in 1870 but
123,931, and in 1880 only 119,686; while of
persons born out of the States, but within the
United States, there were 1,813 less in 1880 than in
1870. These are facts which, even if taken alone,
are of deep significance. Still more striking, however, are some estimates which have been drawn
up for me by a distinguished statistical expert at
Washington, and which show the probable numerical aspect of the race question in the eight old
Slave States in the near future. Several years
ago Professor E. W. Gilliam published a forecast
of the developments of the present situation. His
estimate of the rate of increase of the Southern
whites and negroes was somewhat more alarmist
than that which I am now able to give. The
new estimate is based upon the general, though
not upon the detailed, results of the Census of
1890 ; and as it also makes allowance for the often
alleged imperfections of the Census of 1870, I
think that it may be accepted as, upon the whole,
a better one than that of Mr. Gilliam, or, indeed,
than any that has yet been attempted. I feel
bound to mention Mr. Gilliam's name in connec-

tion with this matter, for his tables have been very widely quoted, and have been made the foundation of much discussion and speculation. I only reject them because I have others which are the results of fuller and later knowledge. Mr. Gilliam's views on some unfortunately less changeable aspects of the race question remain to-day as true and as valuable as when they were committed to paper seven years ago, and I hope to quote them when, after having completed the dry statistical survey of the whole subject, I proceed to deal with the difficulties and dangers of the Southern problem. Here, in the meantime, is my informant's estimate of the white and coloured populations of the Black Belt States in the years 1900 and 1910 respectively:—

	1900.		1910.	
	White.	Coloured.	White.	Coloured.
North Carolina ..	1,010,000	865,000	1,100,000	1,020,000
Virginia	985,000	835,000	1,050,000	965,000
Georgia	1,060,000	1,090,000	1,190,000	1,310,000
Florida	295,000	245,000	380,000	340,000
Alabama	870,000	935,000	1,000,000	1,125,000
Louisiana	582,000	755,000	635,000	915,000
Mississippi	645,000	840,000	750,000	965,000
South Carolina ..	465,000	875,000	510,000	1,055,000
	5,912,000	6,440,000	6,635,000	7,695,000
	12,352,000		14,330,000	

As illustrating the moderation of this estimate, it is worth while adding that Professor Gilliam, writing in 1883, was of opinion that, from 1880 onwards, the whites in the South might be expected to increase at the rate of 2 per cent. per annum, and to double their numbers in thirty-five years, and that the blacks in the South might be expected to increase at the rate of $3\frac{1}{2}$ per cent. per annum and to double their numbers in twenty years. These formulæ would give to the eight old Slave States about 9,390,000 whites in 1915, and about 17,400,000 blacks in 1920. The actual rate of increase is, however, a comparatively unimportant matter. The significant fact of the situation is that in three or four of the eight States the coloured population already outnumbers the white, and that in every one of the remaining four or five States the existing white majority has been for years growing smaller and smaller, and bids fair within a very short period to disappear entirely, and to make place for an overwhelming and ever-growing black majority.

At present, even in South Carolina, which is the "blackest" State in the Union, the white, and the white alone, rules. He seized power, in self-defence it is true, by fraud and violence, and he retains it by deception and intimidation; yet, strange to say, even the most respected and (in ordinary dealings) upright white people of the South excuse and defend this course of procedure; and, stranger still, very many honourable citizens of the North, Republicans as well as Democrats, do not hesitate to declare, " If I were a Southern white man I should act as the Southern white men do." The cardinal principle of the political creed of 99 per cent. of the Southern whites is that the white man must rule at all costs and at all hazards. In comparison with this principle every other article of political faith dwindles into ridiculous insignificance. White domination is a living question that dwarfs tariff reform, protection, free trade, and the very pales of party. The white who does not believe in it above all else is regarded as a traitor and an outcast. The race question is, in the South, the sole question of burning interest. If you be sound on that question you are one of the elect; if you be unsound, you take rank as a pariah or as a lunatic.

After the War of Secession the North complacently folded its hands and announced that the race problem had been for ever disposed of. It soon learned that such had not been precisely the case. Then, after making an ill-advised and spasmodic effort at settlement, it declared that the race problem was no longer its affair, and that it might be left to solve itself. But since

then years have elapsed, and the question still
remains unsettled, paralysing the South, menacing
the whole Union, and liable at any moment to
involve hundreds of thousands of miles of territory
and millions of human lives in a catastrophe
scarcely inferior to that of the great Civil War.
Is it not time, then, for something to be done
towards freeing the South from the incubus of
the situation, and the North from the danger that
lurks still along the line which, less than a generation ago, saw Federal and Confederate striving in
vain to settle this very question ?

It may be asked : Why cannot the South submit itself to the operation of those principles by
which the North is governed ? Why not allow the
majority—no matter what may be its hue—to
rule ?

The answer is that the experiment has been
to some extent tried, and has utterly failed. The
history of the attempt and of the failure is given
in the following chapter. The outlines of that
history must be studied by every one who aspires
to understand the nature and difficulties of the
Southern problem as it exists to-day. I do not,
therefore, apologise for setting forth at some
length the gloomy narrative of one of the most
extraordinary episodes in the modern history of
any civilised country. If I needed further excuse,

I might find it in the fact that my story, though it deals with events of comparatively recent occurrence and of a very terrible character, is unknown to the majority of Englishmen. Even in the North it is now well-nigh forgotten; and only in the long-suffering South are the hideous lessons of it still fully remembered.

CHAPTER II.

THE Civil War ended in 1865, and the Confederacy lay crushed and dead. With it died slavery in the United States. The Slavery Question was, of course, the *fons et origo* of the war, but it was by no means the sole, or even the ostensible, point at issue between North and South. Nor was anything beyond the mere manumission of the slave ever involved in the slavery question. The North did not fight that the manumitted slave might be placed on terms of perfect equality with the white man, or even that he might obtain the franchise. It fought, so far as slavery was concerned, for manumission, and for nothing else; and it gained its point. The point is expressed in the Amendment XIII. to the Constitution, which declares that " neither slavery nor involuntary servitude, except as a punishment for crime, whereof the party shall have been duly convicted, shall exist within the United States or any place subject to their jurisdiction."

c 2

And it may be said at once that there is now
nowhere in the United States any party which
regrets that slavery has been abolished, or which
would restore it to-morrow, even if it were able
to do so by a stroke of the pen. Yet there is,
and always has been, not merely in the South, but
also in the North and West, a very powerful
party which is of opinion that the manumitted
slave and the uneducated negro and coloured man
ought not to be placed on terms of perfect equality
with the white man, and ought not to be permitted to exercise the franchise. Indeed, the
slave's emancipation, as well as his citizenship,
was effected as a tribute to military and political,
rather than to moral, exigencies. Writing to
W. S. Speer, on October 23rd, 1860, Mr. Lincoln
said :—

"I appreciate your motive when you suggest the propriety
of my writing for the public something disclaiming all intention to interfere with slaves or slavery in the States; but in
my judgment it would do no good. I have already done this
many, many times, and it is in print and open to all who
will read."

And, writing to Mr. Lincoln on December 26th
following, Mr. Seward said :—

"I met on Monday my Republican associates on the
Committee of Thirteen, and afterwards the whole Committee.
With the unanimous consent of our section, I offered three

propositions which seemed to me to cover the ground of the suggestion made by you through Mr. Weed, as I understood it. First, that the Constitution should never be altered so as to authorise Congress to abolish or interfere with slavery in the States. This was accepted."

This attitude of the Republican leaders changed as the war went on; but even then the giving to the negro of full political rights and perfect equality was not contemplated. Amendment XIII. says nothing on that head, and Mr. Lincoln, in his last days, expressed himself as opposed to such a wholesale measure. But, the South having been conquered, means had to be devised for keeping it for a time under political subjection, and no means were more obvious or ready to hand than, firstly, a military occupation, with all that such occupation entails; and, secondly, the extension of the suffrage and of the full rights of citizenship to the people who, up to the time of the war, had been slaves. These people, not two or three per cent. of whom possessed the simplest rudiments of education, naturally looked upon the North as a Heaven-sent deliverer, and were in consequence anxious, when they obtained the suffrage, to support their Northern friends. Thus they were Republicans almost to a man. The Southern whites were, and still are, with nearly equal unanimity,

Democrats. In the North, so far as my observation enables me to judge, the Republican party enfolds the majority of the brains and ability of the population. In the South, beyond all doubt, the Democratic party is the party of knowledge and mental power. And in the South, moreover, so far as educated white men are concerned, it is practically the only party. There are Southern Republicans; but they are, almost without exception, negroes, coloured people, or the lowest and most ignorant class of whites.

At first, the process of " reconstructing " the ex-Confederate States was not made to involve the employment of the liberated slave as an agent for the subjection of his former master; but as time went on the black man's obvious utility was perceived. The following sketch will show how the eight old Slave States in which there was, and still is, the largest negro and coloured element, passed from the condition in which they found themselves at the end of the war to the condition in which they are at the present moment. The particulars concerning Alabama are mainly summarised from a paper by Mr. Hilary A. Herbert, member of Congress for that State; those concerning North Carolina from a paper by Mr. Zebulon B. Vance, United States Senator for that State; those concerning South Carolina from a paper by Mr. John J. Hemphill, member of Congress for that State; those concerning Georgia from a paper by Mr. Henry G. Turner, member of Congress for that State; those concerning Florida from a paper by Mr. Samuel Pasco, United States Senator for that State; those concerning Virginia from a paper by Mr. Robert Stiles, a distinguished Virginian; those concerning Mississippi from a paper by Mr. Ethelbert Barksdale, ex-member of Congress for that State; and those concerning Louisiana from a paper by Mr. B. J. Sage. These papers, with others, were collected and published during the past year by Mr. Hilary A. Herbert at Baltimore, under the general title of " Why the Solid South ?"* and they form, I think, the most instructive key that has yet been fitted to the great question, " Why are the United States practically two nations ? " I have had the honour of meeting several of the writers, and I believe them to be all men of uprightness and fairness. I have added numerous illustrative details which have been supplied to me from other trustworthy sources, which, however, I need not here catalogue.

After the close of the war, each of the vanquished States received from the President a

* "Why the Solid South ? or, Reconstruction and its Results." Baltimore : R. H. Woodward and Co. 1890.

provisional governor, who had authority to call a convention to frame a constitution of government. The States soon recognised the new situation. Under the new order of things the suffrage was still confined to white men, and senators and representatives were duly elected, and awaited permission to act. They were almost all Democrats. This fact had its effect upon the Republicans, and when the Thirty-ninth Congress opened in December, 1865, Mr. Thad. Stevens, who thenceforth took the lead in the matter, said:—"According to my judgment, they" (the insurrectionary States) " ought never to be recognised as capable of acting in the Union, or of being counted as valid States, until the Constitution shall have been so amended as to make it what its makers intended, and so as to secure perpetual ascendency to the party of the Union."

Mr. Stevens' plans were two—to reduce the representation to which the late slave-holding States were entitled under the Constitution, and to enfranchise blacks and disenfranchise whites. But even so late as 1865-6 the North was not prepared to grant negro suffrage. Pennsylvania, Ohio, Connecticut, and other States, would have none of it. It was agreed, however, in February, 1866, that neither House should admit any mem-

ber from the late Insurrectionary States until the
report of a joint committee which had been
appointed to consider the question of reconstruction should be received.

This was a declaration of war upon President
Johnson's plan of pacification, but President
Johnson did not give way. He vetoed a Bill to
confer many rights—not including suffrage—
upon the freedmen, because, in his opinion, it
was unconstitutional. Then followed the struggle
over the proposed Amendment XIV. to the Constitution, an amendment which apportioned representatives in Congress upon the basis of the
voting population, and which provided that no
person should hold office under the United States
who, having taken an oath as a Federal or State
officer to support the Constitution, had subsequently engaged in war against the Union.
This struggle led to much bad blood, in spite of
the fact that the amendment in its original form
did not pass.

Still worse feeling was stirred up by the
action of the Freedmen's Bureau agents in the
South. The Freedmen's Bureau had been established in 1865 to act as the guardian of freedmen,
with power to make their contracts, settle their
disputes with employers, and care for them
generally. Many of the agents of this Bureau

traded upon their position, and, with a view to
furthering their own political aspirations, deliberately fomented race hatreds. They widely
disseminated among the freedmen a belief that
the lands of their former owners were, at least to
some extent, to be divided among the ex-slaves;
and, said General Grant, "the effect of the belief
in the division of lands is idleness and accumu-
lation in camps, towns, and cities." A more
salutary lesson would have been that in the sweat
of his face must a man earn his bread; but this
the agents, as a mass, did not teach. On the
contrary, they demoralised the labour situation
in the South, and, later, nearly all of them took
advantage of, and reaped profit from, the demoralisation which they had created. Their ranks
supplied an enormous number of candidates for
office.

In the meanwhile the joint committee on reconstruction was at work. It consisted of twelve
Republicans and only three Democrats; and on the
sub-committee, which collected evidence respecting the condition of Virginia, North Carolina,
South Carolina, Georgia, Alabama, Mississippi,
and Arkansas, there was no Democrat at all.

The situation in those and the other Southern
States was confessedly not good. The ex-Confederate soldiers had returned home demoralised

by defeat, and found four millions of slaves
demoralised by sudden manumission and by the
action of the Freedmen's Bureau agents; and,
naturally, there was much friction between the
races. But the committee's report of the nature
and amount of that friction was greatly exaggerated. As to the State of Alabama, only five
witnesses were examined, all of them being
Republican politicians of notoriously partisan
character. These witnesses had everything to
gain and nothing to lose by "reconstruction";
and, as a matter of fact, when "reconstruction"
followed, one of them became Governor of his
State, a second a Senator in Congress, a third a
permanent official at Washington, a fourth a
Circuit Judge in Alabama, and the fifth a Judge
of the Supreme Court of the District of Columbia.
It may not have been *propter hoc*, but it was
certainly *post hoc*, and the coincidence is suspi-
cious.

Upon the strength of the report the ex-Confederate States were held to be out of the Union.
Their exact *status* remained to be determined by
the voice of the North, as expressed at the polls.
The elections were held in due course; and on
the first Monday in December, 1866, the Republicans came back to the last session of the Thirty-
ninth Congress flushed with victory. They had

a majority of thirty-one in the Senate and of ninety-four in the House.

But President Johnson, with his vetoes, still stood firm ; and "for the purpose of securing the fruits of the victories gained" the impeachment of the President was determined upon. I need not go into the circumstances of that impeachment, the ultimate excuse for which was the dismissal of Mr. Stanton from the Secretaryship of War. Suffice it to say that Congress took steps for " the extension of the suffrage to the coloured race in the district of Columbia, both as a right and as an example."

Mr. Buckalew, of Pennsylvania, discussing the Bill, said, fairly enough, "Our ancestors placed suffrage on the broad common-sense principle that it should be lodged in, and exercised by, those who could use it most wisely, and most safely, and most efficiently to serve the ends for which Government was instituted," and " not upon any abstract or transcendental notion of human rights which ignored the existing facts of social life. I shall not vote to degrade suffrage. I shall not vote to pollute and corrupt the foundations of political power, either in my own State or in any other." On the other hand, Senator Sumner declared, "Now, to my mind, nothing is clearer than the absolute necessity of suffrage for

all coloured persons in the disorganised States."
(This was in reference to an informal understanding that the late Confederate States were to share
the fate of the district of Columbia.) "It will
not," he continued, "be enough if you give it to
those who read and write. You will not in this
way acquire the voting force which you need
there for the protection of Unionists, whether
white or black. You will not secure the new
allies who are essential to the national cause."

The Bill, thus cynically supported, passed;
but on January 7th, 1867, was vetoed by the
President. The Republican majority, however,
was not to be balked. In spite of the facts that
all resistance to Federal authority in the South
had long since ceased, and that, according to a
decision of Mr. Justice Nelson, of the Supreme
Court, States in which the civil government had
been restored under the pacific Presidential plan
were entitled to all the rights of States in the
Union—in spite of these facts Congress solemnly
decided that the war was not over; and in March,
1867, it passed the celebrated Reconstruction Acts,
in face of the President's veto. These Acts
annulled the State Governments then in operation; divided the States into military districts,
and placed them under martial law; enfranchised
the negroes; disenfranchised all, whether pardoned

or not, who had participated in the war against
the Union, if they had previously held any execu-
tive, legislative, or judicial office under the State
or general Government; and provided for the
calling of conventions, the framing and adopting
of State constitutions, and the election of State
officials. In the interim the military commanders
were given absolute power, death sentences only
being subject to the approval of the President.

This action of the Republicans was far from
being in accordance with the just and statesman-
like principles of Lincoln, who, writing in 1862
to Governor Shepley, in Louisiana, said that only
respectable citizens of Louisiana, voted for by
other respectable citizens, were wanted as representatives in Washington. " To send," he continued, " a parcel of Northern men here, elected,
as would be understood, and perhaps justly so, at
the point of the bayonet, would be disgraceful
and outrageous." In less than five years party
spirit had blinded even great Republicans to
these dictates of generosity and far-seeing patriotism. Garfield so far forgot his usually chival-
rous character as to say exultingly, " This Bill
sets out by laying its hands on the rebel governments and taking the very breath of life out of
them; in the next place it puts the bayonet at
the breast of every rebel in the South; in the

next place it leaves in the hands of Congress, utterly and absolutely, the work of reconstruction."

Now, indeed, the ex-Confederate States were about to pay dearly for their faults in the past. They had fought, and had poured forth blood and treasure; they had been beaten, and they had submitted, but they were not forgiven. They had enslaved the black. Henceforth, for a season, the black, ignorant, unscrupulous, dissolute, and corrupt, was to enslave them.

What I have written so far applies equally to all the Southern States. The miserable fortunes of each individual State from the time of the passing of the Reconstruction Acts have next to be followed. I will endeavour to be brief, but no study of the negro question in the United States can, as has been said, be perfect, or even comprehensible, without some allusion to the terrible penalty that was exacted from a brave but vanquished people in and after 1867. The States were one and all Democratic. By June, 1868, eight out of the eleven were represented in both branches of Congress. Of the representatives, all but two were Republicans; of the Senators, not one was a Democrat; and one-half of the whole were Northerners, who had been elected by means such as Mr. Lincoln, in

1862, had declared to be disgraceful and outrageous. In 1871, when all the States had been
reconstructed, the South was represented at
Washington by seventy Republicans and only
fifteen Democrats.

RECONSTRUCTION IN ALABAMA.

In Alabama, as elsewhere, a working and
fairly satisfactory Government had been summarily overthrown by the Reconstruction Acts.
It now made way for a Republican Government
dominated by negroes, most of whom could
neither read nor express an intelligent opinion on
any current topic. The negroes almost to a man
were Republican, and so violent was unreasoning
party feeling among them that a few blacks who
were Democrats were expelled from their
churches. There was a negro majority in the
Convention which was elected in 1867 to frame a
new Constitution ; and, although it was required
that for the ratification of the Constitution a
majority of the registered electors of the State
should vote, the new Constitution was ratified by
Congress, in defiance of the fact that the
necessary majority had not voted. Under the
new Constitution began an era of Republican
control of an avowedly Democratic State, with

twenty-six negroes in the House and one in the
Senate. During this period legislators, as one of
their number is reported to have said, "sold their
votes for prices that would have disgraced a
negro in the time of slavery." Money was obtained for public works, but never legitimately
expended, and the only people to profit were
the Northern "carpet-baggers" and the Southern
negroes, many of whom were not even taxpayers. A state of strife and ill-feeling was
sedulously kept up between the races, and job-
bery and corruption were universal and unveiled.
After the elections of 1872, so outrageous were
the frauds on the part of the managers that both
Democrats and Republicans claimed the victory,
and for a season there were rival Legislatures in
existence. The Democrats, however, submitted,
in presence of United States' troops.

All kinds of most incompetent men were
appointed to judicial positions. For example, the
first judge of the criminal court at Selma was
one Corbin, an old Virginian, who had never
practised law. Its first clerk was Roderick
Thomas, a coloured man, who until after his
manumission was wholly without education.
When Corbin left the Bench, Thomas succeeded
him, and another coloured man, as ignorant as
Thomas, succeeded to the position of clerk.

D

Here is an extract, illustrative of the character of
Corbin, from that eccentric judge's charge to the
grand jury on July 27th, 1874 :—

" Time was, and not very distantly, gentlemen, when this
charge was done up and delivered in grand old style : when
grand old judges, robed in costly black silk gowns and coiffured
with huge old periwigs, swelling out their august personages,
were escorted into the Court-rooms by obsequious sheriffs,
bearing high before them and with stately step their blazoned
insignia of offices. . . . Fair ladies and courtly old dames
of pinguid proportions, in rich and rustling silk brocades,
flocked to grace the Court-room with their enchanting presence
and to hear the august, gowned, and periwigged old judges
ventilate their classic literature and their cultivated oratory in
the grandiloquent old charge."

Corbin quarrelled with his party, which got
rid of him. His characteristic comment was that
the Republicans were " a parcel of pigs; as soon
as one got an ear of corn the others took after
him to get it away."

Such appointments as his were some of the
fruits of ignorant negro dominion in Alabama.
They exasperated the Democrats, who, in spite of
much that is not creditable to them, are, and
ever since the war have been, the most respectable party in the State. In less than seven years
this negro domination rendered the State bank-
rupt and the population furious. The elections
of 1874 were, in consequence, attended by much

regretable fraud and violence, and, by some
means, a Democratic majority was obtained. It
has kept itself in office ever since; it has re-
modelled the Constitution; it has brought back
economy and, I believe, honesty in the administration of the public funds; it has largely reduced the State indebtedness, and it has wholly
restored the public credit. It may have gained
and preserved its object by discreditable means,
but it has not abused its power, and to-day, save
for the black shadow of the Race Question,
Alabama flourishes.

RECONSTRUCTION IN NORTH CAROLINA.

North Carolina fared much as did Alabama.
Under the Reconstruction Acts and Amendment
XIV. her most intelligent voters were proscribed,
and power fell into the hands of plunderers and
adventurers. The result of the voting for the
Constitutional Convention in 1867 was that one
hundred and ten Republicans and only ten Democrats were returned by a notoriously Democratic
State; and the new Constitution of 1868 introduced an era of despotism and fraud. The
negroes were permitted to vote before they were
legally entitled to the suffrage, and in the new
Senate there were thirty-eight Republicans and

D 2

twelve Democrats, while in the House there were
eighty Republicans and forty Democrats. Several
of the negro members of the Legislature were
unable to read. At every opportunity these men
robbed the State and trifled with its credit. There
was open corruption and universal bribery. There
was formed a political " ring," which demanded,
and generally received, 10 per cent. on all appropriations passed by the Legislature. Lavish
entertainments were given and paid for out of
public money. " A regular bar was established
in the Capitol, and it was said that, with somewhat less publicity, some of its rooms were devoted
to the purposes of prostitution. Decency fled
abashed ; the spectacle of coarse, ignorant negroes
sitting at table, drinking champagne and smoking
Havannah cigars, was not uncommon.

"I cannot refrain," continues Mr. Vance,
" from telling a story which I have heard of one,
old ' Cuffy,' who was a member of that body,
and a shining light in the movement of progress
—one who, in the language of Mr. Hoar, had his
' face turned towards the morning light.' A
friend, going to see him one night at his rooms,
found him sitting at a table, by the dim light of
a tallow dip, laboriously counting a pile of money,
and chuckling to himself. ' Why,' said his visitor,
' what amuses you so, Uncle Cuffy?' ' Well,

boss,' he replied, grinning from ear to ear, 'l'se been sold in my life 'leven times, an', fo' de Lord, dis is de fust time I eber got de money.'"

The boldness of the robbers of the State was extraordinary. On one occasion they obtained authority for an issue of bonds to the amount of nearly £3,000,000 sterling, for the construction of a railway. These bonds were all issued, but not so much as a single yard of the line was ever laid down. Yet the people submitted patiently, until what was known as the Schoffner Act was passed. This, under the pretence of suppressing internal disorders, authorised the Governor, at his discretion, to declare any county in a state of insurrection, to proclaim martial law, and to try accused persons by drumhead court-martial. It also authorised the raising of two regiments of troops, one of which was composed of negroes, and the other of which was made up of white desperadoes, under the command of the infamous Kirk. The proceedings under this Act were of such a terrorising nature that the whole country took alarm. Many Republicans, black and white, joined the Democrats; at the elections of 1870, after a shorter reconstruction period than fell to the lot of many other States, the Democrats successfully reasserted themselves, and North Carolina was redeemed. She has not since recovered her financial position, but she bids fair to do so.

So cruelly did South Carolina suffer during the era of reconstruction, and so completely was she abased, that before the period of her sufferings ended she became known as the "Prostrate State." Her best white citizens being disfranchised, she could not make her real voice heard, and, in 1867, the election of delegates to the Convention for the framing of a new constitution for her resulted in the return of sixty-three negroes or coloured people and but thirty-four whites. The latter were, almost without exception, either Northern adventurers or Southern renegades ; the former were, as a body, as ignorant as it is possible to conceive. In 1868 the constitution which had been drawn up by this strange Convention was adopted, chiefly upon the strength of the votes of the negroes who were not then legally enfranchised, but who, nevertheless, were encouraged by the Republican managers to go to the polls.

Under the new constitution a General Assembly was elected. It included seventy-two whites and eighty-five coloured men or negroes, and of the total number one hundred and thirty-six were Republicans and only twenty-one Democrats. All this happened in spite of the fact that Amendment XV. to the United States Constitution, the amendment which conferred the franchise upon the negro, was not ratified until March 30, 1870. General R. K. Scott, of Ohio, an ex-officer of the Freedmen's Bureau, was chosen Governor, and, almost immediately, the black majority, assisted by the white Republican carpet-baggers, began to tyrannise over the white Democrats, and to exploit the State in their own private interests.

An Act passed in 1869 abolished the long-established rule of evidence that all men shall be considered innocent until proved guilty, and expressly directed that if the person whose rights under the Act were alleged to have been denied happened to be coloured, then the burden of proof would be on the defendant; so that any person or corporation named in the Act, if simply accused by a person of colour, was thereby to be presumed to be guilty, and was liable to be subjected to heavy penalties upon this mere accusation, without a particle of proof by the plaintiff or any other witness.

As for the extravagance of the new rulers, it was unlimited. When they first met in legislative assembly, in 1868, they used the same building which the whites had occupied before them, and they furnished it inexpensively. But as soon as they realised their power, they exhibited their luxurious tastes, and furnished anew the legislative halls in the State House. For clocks that had cost 8s. 6d. they substituted clocks that cost £120; for spittoons that had cost 1s. 8d. they substituted spittoons that cost £1 14s.; for benches that had cost 16s. 6d. they substituted crimson sofas that cost £40; for chairs that had cost 4s. 2d. they substituted crimson plush gothic chairs that cost £12; for desks that had cost £2 they substituted desks that cost £35; and for looking-glasses that had cost 16s. 6d. they substituted mirrors that cost £120. The furnishing of the hall of the House of Representatives of this impoverished State cost £19,000. The same hall has recently been very nicely refurnished for £612. At least forty bed-rooms were furnished at the public expense, some of them three times over. A restaurant was also maintained in one of the committee rooms of the Capitol at Columbia, and there officials and their friends and relatives helped themselves, without stint, to food, liquors, and cigars, at the cost of the taxpayer. For six years this restaurant was kept open every day from eight o'clock on one morning until three o'clock on the next. In a single session the restaurant swallowed up £25,000. Nor was this by any means all. In 1873 Mr. J. S. Pike, late United States Minister to Holland, a Republican, and originally a staunch Abolitionist, wrote a little book,* on the situation in South Carolina. His testimony cannot be challenged. He, at least, was no Southern Democrat, full of hatred to "niggers," and to all the works of the North; and the picture that he painted is one which shows corruption, extravagance, and legislative wickedness such as never prevailed even in Hayti in its worst days. Describing "A Black Parliament," he says :—

"Here, then, is the outcome, the ripe, perfected fruit of the boasted civilisation of the South after 200 years of experience. A white community that had gradually risen from small beginnings till it grew into wealth, culture, and refinement, and became accomplished in all the arts of civilisation ; that successfully asserted its resistance to a foreign tyranny by deeds of conspicuous valour ; that achieved liberty and independence through the fire and tempest of civil war, and illustrated itself in the councils of the nation by orators and statesmen worthy of any age or nation—such a community is then reduced to this. It lies prostrate in the dust, ruled over by this strange conglomerate, gathered from the ranks of its own servile population. . . . In the place of this old aristocratic society stands the rude form of the most ignorant

* "The Prostrate State."

democracy that mankind ever saw invested with the functions of government. It is the dregs of the population habited in the robes of their intelligent predecessors, and asserting over them the rule of ignorance and corruption through the inexorable machinery of a majority of numbers. It is barbarism overwhelming civilisation by physical force. . . . We will enter the House of Representatives. Here sit 124 members; of these twenty-three are white men, representing the remains of the old civilisation. . . . These twenty-three white men are but the observers, the enforced auditors, of the dull and clumsy imitation of a deliberative body, whose appearance in their present capacity is at once a wonder and a shame to modern civilisation. . . . The Speaker is black, the clerk is black, the door-keepers are black, the little pages are black, the Chairman of the Ways and Means is black, and the chaplain is coal-black. At some of the desks sit coloured men whose types it would be hard to find outside of Congo ; whose costumes, visages, attitudes, and expressions only befit the forecastle of a buccaneer."

Such were the rulers of a State that then contained over 300,000 white men and women. In 1869 an exclusively coloured militia was organised, and, by the end of 1870, 96,000 men were enrolled in it. To fourteen regiments of these men arms and ammunition were issued before the re-election of General Scott in 1870; they officially attended political meetings and were paid for their services there, and they were confessedly enrolled and used for political purposes. An armed constabulary was maintained for the same objects. On June 25, 1870, J. W. Anderson, a deputy-constable, reported to his chief :— " We can carry the county (York) if we get constables enough, by encouraging the militia, and frightening the poor white men. I am going into the campaign for Scott." And on July 8, 1870, Joseph Crews, a deputy-constable, reported from Laurens county :—" We are going to have a hard campaign up here, and we must have more constables. I will carry the election here with the militia if the constables will work with me. I am giving out ammunition all the time. Tell Scott he is all right here now." Again, testifying before a legislative committee in 1877, J. B. Hubbard, the Chief Constable, said :—

" It was understood that by arming the coloured militia and keeping some of the most influential officers under pay, a full vote would be brought out for the Republicans, and the Democracy, or many of the weak-kneed Democrats, intimidated. At the time the militia was organised, there was, comparatively speaking, but little lawlessness. The militia, being organised and armed, caused an increase of crime and bloodshed in most of the counties, in proportion to their numbers and the number of arms and amount of ammunition furnished them."

Governor Scott spent £75,000 of public money in the advancement of his candidature, and his majority of 30,000 votes was due entirely to terrorism and bribery. In 1871 it

was discovered that the Financial Board had
illegally issued several millions of State bonds,
and there was a movement for the impeachment
of Scott, who was a member of the Board. To
save himself Scott issued three warrants upon
the Armed Force Fund, leaving the amounts
blank, and gave them to two of his political
associates. The warrants were afterwards filled
up for £9,729, and the money was used to bribe
members of the Legislature, the result being that
the Governor escaped. In the meantime, so outrageous was the waste of public money, and so
unabashed the general corruption, that several out-
breaks occurred. These were suppressed by a
suspension in certain counties of the writ of *habeas
corpus ;* but there is no doubt that they represented
chiefly the efforts of honest citizens to protect
themselves when they found that the Government
did not protect them.

Mr. Franklin J. Moses, jun., succeeded General
Scott as Governor, in 1872 ; and under him corruption grew more rampant than ever. Writing
soon after that person had assumed office, Mr.
J. S. Pike said :—

"The whole of the late Administration . . . was a
morass of rottenness, and the present Administration was
born of the corruptions of that. . . . There seems to be
no hope, therefore, that the villainies of the past will be

speedily uncovered. The present Governor was Speaker of the last House, and he is credited with having issued during his term of office over $400,000 (£80,000) of pay certificates, which are still unredeemed and for which there is no appropriation, but which must be saddled on the taxpayers sooner or later. . . . Taxation is not in the least diminished; and nearly $2,000,000 per annum are raised for State expenses where $400,000 formerly sufficed. . . . The new Governor has the reputation of spending $30,000 to $40,000 a year on a salary of $3,500; but his financial operations are taken as a matter of course, and only referred to with a slight shrug of the shoulders. . . . The total amount of the stationery bill of the House for the twenty years preceding 1861 averaged $400 (£80) per annum. Last year it was $16,000 (£3,200). . . . It is bad enough to have the decency and intelligence and property of the State subjected to the domination of its ignorant black pauper multitude, but it becomes unendurable when to that ignorance the worst vices are superadded."

Moses's rule was far worse than Scott's. There was more waste, more corruption, and more lawlessness. In 1874 a committee was appointed to represent the state of affairs to the President; but Moses and his fellows learnt betimes of this intention, and, having misappropriated £500 of public money for the purpose, were able to checkmate the move. It is impossible here to go into details of the various legislative and political scandals of the period. So venal was Moses, and so notoriously did he sell his power, that, more than once, judges announced from the bench their unwillingness to put the people to the expense and trouble of convicting criminals for the Governor to pardon.

Governor D. H. Chamberlain, a well-meaning and honest Republican, succeeded this miscreant in 1874; yet he proved too weak to control his party. Owing to the action of a remnant of Scott's negro militia, a bloody riot occurred in Edgefield county in January, 1875; and in his treatment of this event, as well as in his attempts to lessen the public expenditure, Mr. Chamberlain showed that he was animated by the best desires; but in 1875 his efforts to ensure the purity and integrity of the Bench were circumvented by a conspiracy among his followers; and among the judges then chosen was the infamous ex-Governor Moses. Mr. Chamberlain refused to commission him, and the man never served. The circumstances of his choice, however, aroused the country, and determined the people to oust the Republicans. At the elections of 1876 they chose as their Governor General Wade Hampton, and put Democrats and white men into all official and representative positions. In this election there were fraud and violence on both sides; but, while the Democrats were fighting for their liberty, and almost for their lives, the Republicans were fighting mainly for office alone. And the victors have not, upon the whole, abused their victory. They have introduced administrative economy; they have restored the credit of their State; they have cared for education and general progress; and they have brought back a fair measure of peace and a large one of prosperity.

And here I should add one word more concerning Moses. After his fall from power he became a criminal of the vulgarest character. In 1881 he was sentenced to six months' imprisonment for fraud to the amount of $25; in 1884 he was sentenced to three months' imprisonment for swindling; in 1885 he was sentenced to six months' imprisonment for fraud to the amount of $34; and in the same year he was sent to prison for three years for five other fraudulent transactions. After his release he was arrested for stealing overcoats from the hall of a New York house. He was apparently an incorrigible scoundrel first and last.

In 1877 a committee was appointed by the Legislature of South Carolina to inquire into and report upon the scandals of the period from 1867 to 1876. I cannot resist the temptation of making a few extracts from the report:—

"If the simple statement was made that Senators and Members of the House were furnished with everything they desired, from swaddling clothes and cradle to the coffin of the undertaker, from brogans to chignons, from finest extracts to best wines and liquors, and that all was paid for by the State, it would create a smile of doubt and derision; but when we make the statement, and prove it by several witnesses and by vouchers found in the offices of the Clerks of the Senate and House, all must, with sorrow, admit the truthfulness of the report.

"A. O. Jones, Clerk of the House, testifies that supplies were furnished under the head of 'legislative expenses,' 'sundries,' and 'stationery,' and included refreshments for committee rooms, groceries, clocks, horses, carriages, dry goods, furniture of every description, and miscellaneous articles of merchandise for the personal use of the members.

" It is shown that on March 4, 1872, Solomon furnished the Senate with $1,631 worth of wines and liquors, and on the 7th day of the same month with $1,852 75c. worth.

" Whilst fraud, bribery, and corruption were rife in every department of the State Government, nothing equalled the infamy attending the management of public printing. . . . From 1868 to 1876 the sums paid for public printing amounted to $1,326,589 (£265,318)—a sum largely in excess of the cost of public printing from the establishment of the State Government up to 1868. . . . The public printing in this State cost $450,000 (£90,000) in one year, and ex-ceeded the cost of like work in Massachusetts, Pennsylvania, Ohio, Maryland, and New York by $122,932 (£24,588)."

The Committee gives a list of the names of twenty-two Senators and Representatives who received sums varying from £10 to £1,000 under what was called the " division and silence arrangement," and it also gives a list of those who were bribed to vote for these enormous appropriations. Governor Moses received £4,000, Mr. Cardozo (treasurer) received £2,500, and so on. It is not surprising that under so iniquitous a system the State printing bill, which, during the seventy-eight years ending 1868 had been but £121,800, mounted up in the eight years (1868-76) to £265,318. During the negro-Republican era of reconstruction South Carolina's monthly printing bill averaged £11,133; during General Wade Hampton's administration it averaged £103.

RECONSTRUCTION IN GEORGIA.

In Georgia the reconstruction period was likewise full of fraud and corruption. In one short session the pay and mileage allowances of members and officers of the General Assembly amounted to $979,055, or £195,811, and there were no fewer than one hundred and four clerks, or nearly one clerk to every two members. Between 1868 and 1870 the State debt increased from $5,827,000 to $18,183,000, and the State bonds became almost unmarketable, while all public works either fell to ruin or were "run" by, and mainly for the benefit of, unscrupulous adventurers of the worst type. During

E

his term of three years Governor Bullock, the
Reconstruction Governor, pardoned three hundred
and forty-six offenders against the law, some of
whom actually received pardon before trial.
Indeed, seven pardons before trial were granted
to one man, who pleaded them to seven separate
indictments. The elections of December, 1870,
put an end to this. The Democratic victory was
overwhelming, and, before the Deputies of the
people could confront him, Bullock had resigned
office and fled the State. Since that moment
prosperity has revived.

RECONSTRUCTION IN FLORIDA.

In Florida, the first Reconstruction Governor,
Harrison Reed, very nearly doubled the State
expenditure during his four years of office. Railway and legislative scandals were common. From
Governor downwards every official seemed to be
equally corrupt and equally devoid of patriotism.
On one occasion an Act of the Legislature was
forged; and, armed with it, the Governor claimed,
but failed to obtain, some agricultural land scrip
that was in the hands of the Treasury at Washington. The ballot boxes were tampered with, and
the election returns falsified. In the meantime
the State Treasury was often so empty that even

telegraph charges could not be paid. The second Reconstruction Governor, O. B. Hart, who assumed office in 1873, realised the deplorable condition of affairs, but proved powerless to effect reforms. People were kidnapped, really that they might be unable to vote, but professedly in order that they might appear as witnesses in distant courts of justice. A similar process was, on at least one occasion, applied to members of the State Senate, two of whom were arrested and carried to Jacksonville, in order that they might not imperil by their votes the nefarious schemes of their Republican colleagues. The elections of 1876 placed the Democrats in power and introduced a new and more reputable era.

RECONSTRUCTION IN VIRGINIA.

During the reconstruction period Virginia's sufferings were less painful and considerably briefer than were those of most of the other old slave States with which I am dealing. Such misfortunes as she experienced were attributable, nevertheless, to causes exactly the same as those which brought South Carolina to the lowest depths of misery and degradation. In Virginia, as elsewhere, the reconstruction laws disfranchised the majority of the best native whites and

E 2

handed over the country to the tender mercies of ignorant blacks, prompted by unscrupulous carpet-baggers. Yet in Virginia the process known as reconstruction seems to have been singularly uncalled for save as a purely party measure. It was not needed for the protection of the negroes. Professor Alexander Johnston, in the "Cyclo-pædia of Political Science," calls attention to the conspicuous equity of the Virginia statute, made after the war but before reconstruction, for the regulation of contracts between blacks and whites. Reconstruction was needed only for the preserva-tion of Republican power. It ended in 1870, but while it lasted it had a very bad effect upon all the institutions of the State, and especially upon the judiciary. Says Mr. Robert Stiles :— "The writer has appeared in a circuit court of Virginia before a bench upon which sat a so-called Judge, who had the day before been a clerk in a village grocery store, and who was not better fitted for the dignity and duty devolved upon him than the average grocery clerk would be."

RECONSTRUCTION IN MISSISSIPPI.

In Mississippi the period was much longer and much more severe and stormy. It was Mr. John Q. Adams, of Massachusetts, who, describing the treatment during this time of the vanquished and resigned Southerners, said that the Northerners scorned the protests of the ex-Confederates, "repelled their aid, insulted their misery, and inflicted on them an abasement which they felt to be intolerable in posting over them their slaves of yesterday to secure their pledge of submission to the Constitution of the United States." The South, therefore, was by no means alone in feeling that she was aggrieved.

In Mississippi, as in other States, a Convention met after the passing of the Reconstruction Acts to draw up a new State Constitution. The Convention was of the usual "black and tan" complexion, and in the qualities of ignorance, corruption, and depravity was almost all that the imagination can conceive. "It was," says Mr. Ethelbert Barksdale, "a fool's paradise for the negroes, who undertook to perform what they were incapable of doing; and, as to their mercenary white leaders, the stream of purpose which ran through all their actions was plunder and revenge. Not one of the authors and abettors of the plan was actuated by a higher motive than party success. Not one of them believed that it would promote the restoration of the Union to substitute the rule of knaves and negroes for the State Governments which they had overthrown.

They knew the depravity of the white renegades whom they had commissioned to do this work, and they knew, to employ the language of a Northern statesman and Union soldier, that 'in the whole historic period of the world the negro race had never established or maintained a Government for themselves.'"

The Convention was very deliberate in its action. Its members lived in a state of luxury unknown to their previous habits. They voted themselves $10 (£2) a day, and paid their innumerable hangers-on correspondingly high wages; and, although the body cost about £100,000 sterling while it sat, it would have cost far more but for the inexorable attitude of the commanding general, who, in the interregnum, was practically dictator.

The Constitution which the Convention drew up was promptly rejected at the polls, and was only ratified in a modified form upon the holding of a second election in 1869. As originally devised it would have excluded half the intelligent white population from all offices, and would even have actually and permanently disfranchised anyone who during the war had charitably contributed to the relief of sick and suffering Confederate soldiers.

The first election under the Amended Consti-

tution returned a Legislature four-fifths composed
of negroes and carpet-baggers, and the negroes
had a majority. The immediate consequences
were that corruption began to regulate every
public and legislative transaction, and that the
State started on a career which led it with daily
accelerating speed in the direction of ruin.
Within six years 6,400,000 acres of land were
adjudged forfeited for non-payment of the taxes
which were necessary to support the extravagance
and folly of the ruling clique. Thenceforward,
until, at least, these lands were redeemed, taxation
fell with correspondingly increased weight upon
the rest of the unfortunate State. And so matters
went from bad to worse until, after years of
tyranny, waste, and extravagance on the part of
their governors, the whites could submit no
longer.

From a taxpayers' petition addressed to the
Legislature on January 4th, 1875, I extract the
following :—

"To show the extraordinary and rapid increase of taxation
imposed on this impoverished people, these particulars are
cited :—In 1869 the State levy was 10 cents on the hundred
dollars of assessed value of lands. For the year 1871 it was
four times as great. For 1872 it was four times as great.
For the year 1873 it was eight and a half times as great. For
the year 1874 it was fourteen times as great. . . . In

many counties the increase in the county levies has been still greater."

At this crisis Mr. George E. Harris, a Republican ex-Attorney-General and member of Congress, wrote:—" The people are in a state of exaspera- tion, and in their poverty and desperation they are in arms against the burden of taxes levied and collected on their property." But the petition was laughed at by those who were profiting by the misery of the citizens. The people, there- fore, roused themselves, and, partially, it may be, by violence and fraud, but wholly in self- defence, rescued the State at the elections of 1875 from its abasement. Since then there has been no important break in the steady financial, agri- cultural, educational, and industrial improvement of Mississippi.

RECONSTRUCTION IN LOUISIANA.

Louisiana, alas, fared much worse than Missis- sippi—worse, in fact, than any of the old slave States; for even in South Carolina the agony was not so bloody.

The Constitutional Convention of 1867 was elected on a registration list which had been so manipulated as to show only 45,218 white voters to 84,436 black ones; and at the legislative elections of 1868 the successful candidates were chiefly negroes. Indeed, in the Senate there were but about half a dozen whites.

To the summit of this mass of ignorance and corruption a creature named Henry C. Warmoth at once climbed. By arts which can best be compared with those of the political schemer in a burlesque, he had already ingratiated himself with the negroes; and he had little difficulty in inducing his *protégés* to make him the first Reconstruction Governor of Louisiana.

Warmoth originally went to Louisiana in the Federal Army, from which he is said to have been dismissed for good cause. He should appear in history as one of the very worst of the carpet-baggers; yet he was a man of, in some respects, a remarkable character. From his earliest assumption of power he took measures not merely to render himself supreme, but also to render himself irremovable. He was "inaugurated" in July, 1868. Democratic members of the Legislature were, with very few exceptions, excluded by the operation of a test oath imposed by the majority; all election machinery and the disposal of nearly all important offices were entrusted to the hands and sole will of the Governor; and a Board of Registration was appointed, the object of which was to ensure that elections should result favourably to the party in power. Warmoth, whenever he made a considerable appointment, adopted the precaution of simultaneously obtaining from the appointee a resignation in blank; so that rebellious or troublesome officials could always be summarily got rid of by the simple act on the part of the Governor of filling up the blank forms. So complete in time became Warmoth's system that, says Mr. B. J. Sage, " a practically unanimous people could not have driven the Republicans out, save by a popular uprising."

Of the members of the Legislature only ten among the dominant party were taxpayers; and, consequently, the House was not in the slightest degree of sympathy with the people, who soon began to be burdened with a taxation such as had before been undreamt of. Corruption and bribery reigned supreme, " and the knaves, to avoid any possible danger, refused to pass any bribery law, so that it was no crime to bribe a public official." To assist himself and his fellows in controlling elections, Warmoth raised what was in fact, though not in name, a standing army, and subsequently a small fleet; and he caused the establishment in all parishes of Republican newspaper organs, to the conductors of which was given a monopoly of printing the laws and public advertisements. The State expenditure rose to five times its normal level ; the cost of the short session of 1871 amounted to £1,230 sterling per legislator; and the State debt, of course, increased rapidly and alarmingly, until proportionately to the population it became, within only a year and a half, very much larger than that of any State in the Union. Bonds were issued for all kinds of fraudulent objects—many at a rate as high as 8 per cent. ; and all sorts of valuable privileges and franchises were given away to the favourites of the men in power. In fact, the State was plundered wholesale and in every direction. It is calculated that Louisiana was the loser in these years of the equivalent of about £24,000,000 sterling, or of more than half the total estimated wealth of the State.

Warmoth's own share of the spoils was large, but its exact amount can never be ascertained. Up to the time of his accession the average printing expenses of the State had been about $37,000 (£7,400 a year). During the first two years and a half of Warmoth's rule the New Orleans *Republican,* in which he was the principal shareholder, received $1,140,881 (£228,170) for public printing. Warmoth also took upon himself the appointment of the judges—from whom he exacted the usual blank resignations; and thus

with an army, a navy, a press, a bench, a legislature, and election managers all securely, as he
believed, tethered to his chariot, he was absolute
dictator.

He found his justification in the elections of
1870, which went exactly as he willed them to go.
Not even Lopez in Paraguay was more powerful
than Warmoth in Louisiana. "But," says Mr.
Sage, "over the spoils arose the inevitable quarrel,
and the two factions that formed went heartily
into their only good work, which was to acquaint
Louisiana and the world with their rascalities
and infamy, and make manifest the gross wrong
of Congressional reconstruction." For over two
years the Warmothites and the anti-Warmothites
fought, often in arms, frequently with much
bloodshed; and in 1872-73 the State was in a
condition of disgraceful anarchy, which was in
nowise ended by the substitution of Pinchback,
the Lieutenant-Governor, for Warmoth, and by
the impeachment of the latter; for by that time
another Governor, who claimed to have been
properly elected, was in the field in the person of
Mr. W. P. Kellogg. Kellogg was sustained by
United States troops; but, although there were
many riots and much bloodshed on his behalf, he
was never popularly recognised. In one riot
alone sixty-three persons were killed.

Kellogg was worse even than Warmoth had been. In 1874 the whites organised themselves for their protection under the style of the White League. Their attempt to arm themselves led to a bloody battle at New Orleans, in which forty people were killed and 100 wounded. Immediately afterwards Kellogg was overthrown; but he was re-seated by the Federal forces. At the 1874 elections the Democratic whites again swept the State; but Warmoth's cunningly devised Returning Board, which still existed, neutralised the results by summarily rejecting nearly half the successful opposition candidates, and by thus manufacturing another Republican Legislature. Indeed, a number of Democratic members of the House were actually arrested by Federal troops. A Congressional Committee, it is true, afterwards recognised the illegality of these acts, and reinstated a majority of the Democrats, but the policy of the committee did not reconcile the State with Kellogg and with his numerous other enormities. For example, the Governor illegally arrested between 500 and 600 persons at various times, generally on blank warrants; and in every instance in which any of these cases were investigated in Court the charges were dismissed.

The struggle of 1874 had not satisfied Kellogg that there was a point beyond which he should

not go in his requests for Federal assistance. He
determined to make further requests, with a view
to securely intrenching his party during the
elections of 1876. Once more, however, and in
spite of wholesale bribery on the other side, the
Democrats swept the State ; and again the results
were neutralised by the operations of the old
infamous Returning Board. Renewed anarchy,
with two Governors and two Governments,
followed. One Government—that of Packard,
the Republican leader—was unable, nevertheless,
to exercise even a vestige of authority outside
the State House, which, crowded with people,
lay in a state of siege, in spite of the fact that
small-pox had broken out there. Packard waited
for the active Federal support which had never
been refused to Kellogg, but he waited in vain ;
and when, after months of hesitation, the President
withdrew the National troops, Packard and his
Government collapsed. Governor Nicholls, a
Democrat, then assumed full authority ; and from
that day Louisiana has formed part of the " solid "
Democratic South.

    And here let it not be forgotten that public
gambling and public lotteries owed their establishment in Louisiana to Warmoth. The gambling
has since been abolished ; the Louisiana lottery,
owing to its having been granted a twenty-five

years' charter, still exists to remind the world of the evil methods of the period of reconstruction. Warmoth himself said of the Legislature which he had caused to be elected in 1870:—" There is but one honest man in it," and to a delegation he cynically remarked, " Corruption is the fashion ; I do not pretend to be honest, but only as honest as anybody in politics."

I might also trace the history of reconstruction in Tennessee, in West Virginia, in Missouri, and in Arkansas ; but I am chiefly confining my attention to those Southern States which constitute the " Black Belt "—the district, that is, throughout which blacks and whites are nearly evenly balanced, and in which there are particular commonwealths containing more blacks than whites. Moreover, on this branch of the subject I have written enough, I believe, to show reason, if not to show excuse, for the political feeling which occupies the first place in the heart of every Southern white man.

That feeling is, by itself, a political creed stronger than the creed of Republican or of Democrat ; and it may be thus formulated. You have freed our slaves, and, far from regretting, we rejoice in what you have done. Without properly consulting us, you have given those ex-slaves the suffrage and civil rights. There, we think, you have greatly erred. While we will admit that some negroes and coloured people are fit to exercise the suffrage, we are of opinion that the vast majority of them, owing as well to natural lack of mental ballast as to ignorance, are incapable of exercising the suffrage to their own best welfare, to the benefit of the white people among whom they live, and to the general advantage of the nation. Apart from this opinion of ours, and quite regardless of the question whether that opinion be sound or not, we are steadfastly determined never again to submit to any form, direct or indirect, of negro government. We have experienced a form of such government during the Reconstruction Era. In those days the chief sufferers were ourselves, and the chief gainers were, not the negroes, who, like machines, registered the desires of their patrons, but the unscrupulous whites who exploited the negroes. We intend, therefore, to risk no more of that kind of thing. Here and there the negroes may be more numerous than we whites. It must make no difference. The white must rule, no matter at what cost. You shall never again, while we exist, compel us to relinquish that determination. Our view does not, it may be, accord with the principles of your Amendment

XV., but it accords with our ideas of the *minimum* of social comfort and security, and we intend steadfastly to adhere to it, even if adherence should cost us blood and treasure and much more that we hold dear. You Northerners have never known any form of negro domination, and have never been in danger of it. Indeed, you know little about the negro. We have to live with him, and we are familiar with his failings as well as with his virtues. Our knowledge tells us that it would be suicidal folly to entrust ourselves, our families, and our fortunes to his political discretion. You think otherwise; but do not, we pray you, ever attempt to make us practise in all their fulness your very humane theories. We would rather die at once. Congress, we know, once passed a Civil Rights Bill, which directed "that all persons within the jurisdiction of the United States should be entitled to the full and equal enjoyment of the accommodations, advantages, facilities, and privileges of inns, public conveyances on land or water, theatres, and other places of amusement, subject only to the conditions and limitations established by law, and applicable alike to citizens of every race and colour, regardless of any previous condition of servitude." That was very well in theory, but the Act has been held by the United States

F

Supreme Court to be unconstitutional, and, in any case, you must never ask us to accept it. There are occasions when we cannot admit that whites and blacks are equal.

The above position is one upon which the whites of the South are, as I convinced myself during my stay and inquiries here, practically unanimous. It is a position of danger, for it is a position of covert, if not open, hostility to the spirit of laws of the Union. A strict and rigid enforcement of those laws, supposing that it could be attempted, would, there is no doubt, create an exceedingly grave crisis. On the other hand, there is, or may be, danger in the fact that the negro as a citizen does not get all that to which he is legally entitled. How he is deprived of very much that the law affects to give him will be the subject of the next chapter.

CHAPTER III.

THE main outlines of the rights of the negro in the United States are laid down in Amendments XIII., XIV., and XV. to the American Constitution. Says Amendment XIII., "Neither slavery nor involuntary servitude, except as a punishment for crime whereof the party shall have been duly convicted, shall exist within the United States, or any place subject to their jurisdiction." Says Amendment XIV., "All persons born or naturalised in the United States, and subject to the jurisdiction thereof, are citizens of the United States and of the State wherein they reside. No State shall make or enforce any law which shall abridge the privileges or immunities of citizens of the United States; nor shall any State deprive any person of life, liberty, or property without due process of law, nor deny to any person within its jurisdiction the equal protection of the laws." And, says Amendment XV., "The right of the citizens of the United

F 2

States to vote shall not be denied or abridged by the United States, or any State, on account of race, colour, or previous condition of servitude." Such is roughly the American charter of the black and coloured man's liberties.

The Civil Rights Bill, passed by Congress in 1875, went further, and, as I have said, declared that " All persons within the jurisdiction of the United States shall be entitled to the full and equal enjoyment of the accommodations, advantages, facilities, and privilege of inns, public conveyances on land or water, theatres, and other places of amusement, subject only to the conditions and limitations established by law, and applicable alike to citizens of every race and colour, regardless of any previous condition of servitude." But this measure was held by the United States Supreme Court to be unconstitutional ; and I only again cite its first section here in order to show, in all completeness, what the negro in America wants and is struggling for, and what his most enthusiastic friends in the North would give him if they had it in their power to give.

It is because he is not given these rights, and because some of the rights which are given to him in law are withheld from him in practice, that the Race Question is to-day one of towering importance in America. If the American white were able to frankly make up his mind to accept the negro as in all respects his political and social equal, the whole question would vanish, and the two races might, in course of time, become one. But the American white, it is absolutely certain, will never adopt this solution of the difficulty. He will not frankly accept the negro as his equal at the polls, in society, in the court of law, or in the school. He holds that the negro is physically and intellectually inferior in the scale of humanity; and he points, with a gesture that forbids argument, to the differences that exist between the Caucasian and the Caucasian's "brother in black."

Am I, he asks, to admit my equality with a being who more nearly approaches the quadrumana than does any other member of the human family; with a being whose arms are, on an average, two inches longer than mine? Am I to admit my equality with a being whose facial angle is about 70 deg., while mine is about 82 deg.? Am I to admit my equality with a being the average weight of whose brain is ten ounces less than that of people of my own family? Is it a matter of insignificance that he is black while I am white; that his eyes have a yellowish sclerotic coat; that his nose is short, depressed, and dilated; that he has high and prominent check-bones; that his cranium is much thicker than mine; that he has a low instep and a " lark heel "; that his head is covered not with hair but with wool of nearly flat section; that

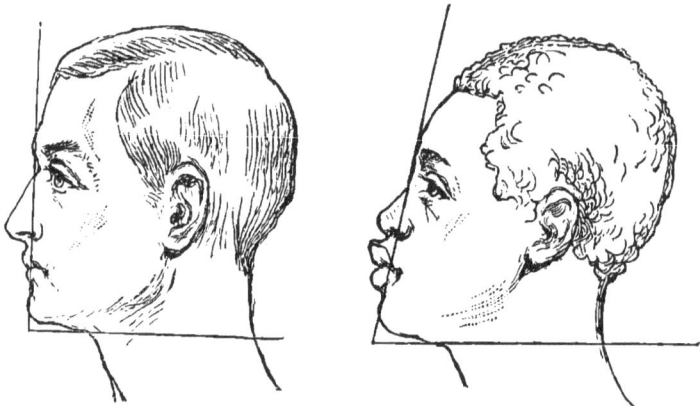

FACIAL ANGLES OF THE WHITE AND NEGRO RACES.

his skin is thicker than mine, and that it is velvety and emits a characteristic odour; that his frame, owing to structural peculiarities, is not as erect as mine; or that the cranial sutures of the negro close up much earlier than those of the white man?

These points of difference, and many more, are ever before the eye and in the mind of the American white in the South. I am not concerned to say whether or not the white man pays exaggerated attention to them. I can only declare that, influenced, rightly or wrongly, by his observations and his prejudices, the white Southerner has impregnably determined that, in spite of anything that Constitutional Amendments and State legislation may hint to the contrary, the negro on American soil occupies an inferior position, and that he must never be allowed to trespass beyond it.

I have already incidentally mentioned that the illegal repression of the black is openly defended by Americans who, in the ordinary affairs of life, take rank as men of honour. Mr. George William Curtis, writing in *Harper's Weekly* in June, 1887, said :—

"What is the Southern question? It is essentially one of the gravest and most vital that can concern any community, for it is substantially the question whether where the coloured vote is largely in the majority, and is cast all together, the community shall be placed under the government of its most ignorant class, recently emancipated from a dehumanising slavery, and led by unscrupulous chiefs. The pitiless cruelty of slavery was not a good school for the exercise of political supremacy in an otherwise highly civilised community, and the situation in some parts of the Southern States is one which, could it be reproduced in the Northern States, would not be tolerated. Relief would be sought and found under law or over law, and that is what is done in such communities in the Southern States. There is plainly a deprivation of rights conferred by law. But would any humane and intelligent

Republican say that the power of the United States should be employed to compel submission to an endless rule like that of Moses in South Carolina?"

And the Boston *Herald*, one of the most respectable of Northern newspapers, candidly tells its New England readers that if they lived in the South they would entertain the same views about the negroes as the Southern whites do. It explains very thoroughly the race prejudice, which is prevalent with all white races, and particularly with the Anglo-Saxon, and which has kept the Anglo-Saxon race pure and has preserved its institutions, civilisation, and free government. Says the *Herald* on this subject :—

" The treatment accorded to coloured races by white men, especially representatives of the Anglo-Saxon race, has never been of a kind to call forth commendations, and yet it may be said that this almost universal display of inhumanity indicates that it is a necessary feature of race development. Our Western countrymen believe that the only good Indian is a dead Indian ; our Southern countrymen believe that the negro is a person who cannot be allowed political and social equality, but must be kept in an inferior condition. We in the North, who have nothing to fear from Indians and with whom the negro is an exception, raise our voices in protest at such barbarity. And yet our forefathers, who were, perhaps, quite as conscientious persons as we are, did not hesitate to undertake a war of extermination against the Indians, and they even held views concerning the negro quite different from those which we entertain.

THE EX-SLAVE AS HE IS.

"In fact, human nature is such that the chances are altogether in favour of the supposition that, if the people of New England could be transported to the North-Western States and Territories, and our fellow citizens of those districts brought back to New England, we should soon have those who now entertain philanthropic views concerning the Indians crying out for their speedy extermination, while those who now regard them as obstacles to civilisation, to be brushed out of the way as soon as possible, would come, looking at them from a perspective of 2,000 miles, to regard them as men and brothers, deserving of kind and equitable treatment. We dare say that the removal of the white people of the North to the Southern States and the transfer of the Southern people to the north of Mason and Dixon's line would be attended with the same reversal of opinions respecting the negro question—that is, the manner in which these race problems are regarded is largely a matter of geographical location."

The Atlanta *Constitution* thus excuses the attitude of the whites. Is there, it asks, a State in the North in which if, as in Mississippi, 181,000 negro voters, of whom 145,000 are unable to read or write, were to-day settled, the white people would be or could be divided under any pretence or by any power ? Is there a Northern State in which, although, as in Mississippi, there were only 121,000 white voters to oppose them, this host of black illiterates could capture and maintain the control of affairs under any pretext or by any power ? Could this be done in Indiana, or in Ohio, and especially could it be done if, as in

Mississippi, the hideous and sickening pages of
the carpet-bag era, by showing what these people
did do when the whites were united against them,
gave appalling suggestions of what they would do
if the whites were divided? Iowa has about
the voting population of Georgia, say 320,000.
If 130,000 of these voters were negroes, of whom
100,000 were illiterate (to say no worse), is there
any sane man who believes, or any fair man who
will assert, that the white people of Iowa would
not so unite as to hold control of their affairs, and
remain so united, in all despite? Would any
political ambition, or could any external force, so
divide the whites as to make it possible for a considerable minority of their number, by deluding
the ignorant and bribing the corrupt of the negroes,
to hold the reins of government?

Nor can it be denied that, in practice, many
of the most negrophil Northerners have as little as
possible to do with the black, and, indeed, systematically treat him as an inferior. A Republican
Congress twenty years ago forced negro suffrage
upon the South, and at the same time established
it in the District of Columbia. Six years' experience of it in Columbia was sufficient, and to get
rid of it a Republican Congress obliterated suffrage
altogether there, amid the hearty amens of Republican property holders in Washington. There

are three Senators now in Congress—Messrs.
Edmunds and Morrill, of Vermont, and Mr. Sherman, of Ohio—who twenty years ago assisted
might and main to burden the South with negro
suffrage. These three are among the foremost in
advocating Southern fairness towards the negro.
Indeed, Mr. Sherman is the author of a propo-
sition in this direction which for stringency goes
far ahead of anything previously suggested. Yet
all three of these Senators, who are large property
holders in Washington, voted to disestablish negro
suffrage in Washington fifteen years ago, and
not one of them would for one moment listen to
any suggestion to revive it.

The attitude of the Southern white towards the
negro is, nevertheless, not exactly an unkind one.
It is rather that of a magisterial guardian. Within certain limits, the negro is no longer " kept
down." Far from seeking to condemn him to
ignorance and stagnation, the white man contributes, and contributes generously, to the
negro's mental, physical, and moral advancement. He freely provides his ex-slave with
facilities for education, with medical care in
seasons of sickness, and with opportunities for
religious instruction. Indeed, in these directions,
he does for the black man a great many good
deeds which the black man never dreams of

trying to do for himself. But this is, I think, mainly because the white systematically regards the black as a child. And in this the white is certainly justified. No one who has associated much with the negro race can have failed to have remarked that in the natural time of childhood the negro is apparently as vivacious and as intelligent as the white. With the approach of puberty, however, the two races begin to betray marked intellectual divergence. The white steadily progresses in intelligence; the black stops short; so that, a few years afterwards, the latter is by comparison dull, stupid, and indolent, though still frivolous, affectionate, good-natured, and mischievous. I speak, of course, of the average negro, and more especially of the full-blooded one. There are exceptions, but they are few. As a rule the grown negro, even if he have received a better education than the majority of his fellows, is in mind always a child. The uneducated grown negro is invariably of this characteristic nature; and he is often charmingly simple and devoid of evil. But, on the other hand, he is quite as often full of the worst vices and passions. Into this, however, I will not go at present, my immediate purpose being rather to show how the negro is treated by his white fellow-citizens than to indicate the effect that is being produced upon the South by the existence in it of an enormous, and in many localities an overwhelming, negro population.

According to law, the American negro has at the polls exactly the same rights and privileges as the American white man. But the concession was made to the negro without the full and free consent of the Southern white, and in consequence the Southern white has always grudged it, and has very rarely allowed it to be fully exercised. There was a time, as I have endeavoured to show, when the Southern white was prevented by *force majeure* from greatly interfering with the negro's action at the ballot-boxes; but since the days of Reconstruction the Southern white man has been supreme in his own States, and his will has ever been that the negro shall not be a significant factor in politics. At first the white enforced his will with the rifle and the revolver. In many places the negro could not approach the ballot-box without risking his life, and so he stayed away. There were " rifle clubs," and, in Texas and Virginia, there was the Ku-Klux Klan, an organisation of whites of good position who were determined, no matter how much blood it might cost, to make the coloured people " behave themselves." Then followed the less violent but not less reprehensible

recourse to " tissue-ballots." " Let the negroes
vote if they will," was the word; " we will
stultify their action by fraud, which is safer
than force." And so it happened that, as in
South Carolina, although the negro majority
trooped to the polls and voted Republican to a
man, the returning officers found that, almost
without exception, the men who were elected
were Democrats.

The infamous trick was easily managed. In
America the voter is, in most places, required to
register, and to produce his registration certificate
upon recording his vote. He votes by depositing
in the ballot-box a printed ticket, or ballot. This
ticket simply bears the names of the favoured
candidates for vacant offices, and, although it
now has to be of certain prescribed dimensions and
colour, its form used to be very much dependent
upon the tastes and idiosyncrasies of the party
leaders who supplied it to the electors. In the
" tissue-ballot " days fraudulent party leaders
caused it to be printed upon the very thinnest of
tissue-paper, so that the thickness of, say, twenty-
five tissue-tickets did not much exceed that of an
ordinary piece of writing-paper. These tickets
were entrusted to unscrupulous voters of the right
political complexion. The ballots, before being
deposited, had to be folded, but only lightly

folded; and thus, when an expert fraudulent voter folded his twenty-five tissue-tickets together and gave them a gentle flip as he dropped them into the box, the papers flew open and apart, and at once assumed a comparatively innocent appearance. Upon the close of the poll the ballots were counted and their number was compared with that of the registered electors who had voted at that booth. There was found to be a large excess of ballots; whereupon all the papers were returned to the box, and an election manager, in accordance with precedent, undertook the duty of withdrawing sufficient ballots to make the remainder tally with the number of voters who had polled. If, as was generally the case, the manager was fraudulent, he took care to draw out only thick tickets. If, as may have sometimes happened, he was honest, he took the tickets as they came, thick and thin indifferently. But in either event the party that used "tissue-ballots" naturally gained an immense advantage. If the negroes—against whom almost exclusively this device was employed—suspected and protested, revolvers were exhibited by the other side.

Such a revelation as this may appear incredible to British readers, but it by no means exhausts the villainies of American politics as they are displayed at the polls, even at this day; and

Americans themselves seem to accept such things as matters of course. Mr. John James Ingalls, one of the United States Senators for Kansas, excited no great surprise or repulsion when he recently declared, " The purification of politics is an iridescent dream; the Decalogue and the Golden Rule have no place in a political campaign." Mr. Ingalls is a Republican. Republicans, however, it is but fair to say, are not monopolists of fraud. A normally respectable Southern newspaper, the Charleston *News and Courier*, during the last campaign, coolly gave to its readers the following conspicuously printed piece of advice:—" Go to the polls to-day. Vote early, vote often, vote straight." (November 4, 1890.) And I am bound to admit that the counsel was acted upon. But of that anon.

Concurrently with the use of " tissue-ballots," the practices of " counting in " and " counting out" were resorted to, or, in other words, false returns were made. Again, the registration certificates of the ignorant and often careless coloured voters were frequently stolen or purchased for ridiculous sums by whites. The regular price used to be fifty cents, or a pint of whisky.

Another favourite device was, and still is, deception. The majority of coloured voters cannot read, and since, at most American elections, there are several " tickets " to be voted for—as, for example, a State ticket, a county or municipal ticket, and a Federal ticket—there is generally plenty of opportunity for Sambo to go wrong. With the assistance of a learned friend, he selects such tickets as he may, in his political wisdom, desire to deposit. He also assures himself as to the relative positions of the various ballot-boxes in the booth. Then, with the State ticket between his forefinger and thumb, the county ticket between his forefinger and second finger, and the Federal ticket between his second and third fingers, and in the happy belief that the State box is on the extreme right, the county box in the middle, and the Federal box on the extreme left, he enters the booth to do his civic duty. In the meantime the managers inside have deliberately changed the position of the boxes. They are legally bound to indicate each box if they be asked to do so; but, even if they comply with the letter of the requirement, Sambo inevitably gets his papers confused, and ends by depositing them wrongly, and so spoils his vote. In practice, the managers, as often as not, either do not indicate the boxes or indicate them wrongly. They are all labelled, but when Sambo is illiterate the labels are meaningless to him.

G

In a speech delivered on July 30th, 1888, Governor John P. Richardson, of South Carolina, openly and frankly defended this practice. Said he :—

"The great problem which God has given us to solve is not yet solved. We have now the rule of a minority of four hundred thousand over a majority of six hundred thousand. No army at Austerlitz, Waterloo, or Gettysburg could ever be wielded like that mass of six hundred thousand people. The only thing which stands to-day between us and their rule is a flimsy statute—the *eight-box law*—which depends for its effectiveness upon the unity of the white people."

In a speech delivered a few days later Governor Richardson again declared :—

"But there is one thing more which the Democracy has to do, and that is to solve the problem of how a minority of four hundred thousand people shall rule for the advancement of the State and the people at large. There are to-day many people who think that the eight-box law could be disposed of, but I tell you that on it depends the salvation of the State. It amounts to an educational qualification for suffrage. None of us can forget the election trials which took place in this city, when a native South Carolinian was the prosecutor against his own people. But if he was the Cicero, we had yet the Demosthenes to meet him, and the gifted Youmans arose, and we saved our comrades by the skin of their teeth. Be careful, my friends, of the eight-box law. Some have said that we could control by simple Anglo-Saxon manhood, but this is only a beautiful theory, and would be dangerous in practice. I have an abiding faith in the onward progress of humanity, and I believe it is the eternal law of God that this land shall be controlled by the Anglo-Saxon race."

The *eight-box law* is the statute which provides a separate box for each ticket, township, county, State, Congressional, Electoral, &c. Every voter must approach these boxes alone, and no one, unless asked, is allowed to tell him where a particular ticket belongs. If he cannot read he cannot, without assistance, distribute his tickets, and, by the law, all that are put into the wrong box are void.

Senator Eustis, of Louisiana, at about the same time publicly asserted that the whites of Louisiana, in spite of the law, would rule by might, and as for the rest of the country it was none of Louisiana's business.

The vulgar devices of making voters drunk and of temporarily restraining their personal liberty are not wholly neglected; but these are troublesome methods, and the easier ones are found by experience to have all the hoped-for effect. Indeed, in many districts, the negro now seems to recognise that his vote, should he deposit it, will not be allowed to count, and he therefore stays at home. In other districts he votes still; but the whole business is a sad farce. And of this I have some personal knowledge.

On November 4th, 1890, I was present at a

G 2

voting place at Mount Pleasant in South Carolina.
The whites were voting for Tillman, the Farmers'
Alliance candidate, for Governor. A small dis-
sentient body of whites and the whole body of
negroes were voting for Haskell, the Democratic-
Republican Coalition candidate. The district is a
very black one, one of the blackest in the State,
and its vote was much counted upon by the
Haskell party. Overnight, therefore, the Till-
manites tried, but in vain, to destroy the booth ;
and on the day of the election they adopted a
modification of the old " tissue-ballot " trick,
using, however, ordinary instead of tissue-ballots.
Two hundred and forty-four persons voted at this
particular booth. When one of the boxes was
opened it was found to contain a largely excessive
number of ballots ; the exact number was, if I
recollect rightly, 477. The surplus 233 papers
were cast out by the managers, some of whom
were shrewdly suspected of being parties to the
conspiracy, and the result of the poll in that
precinct was decided by the verdict of the
remainder. Nor was this the only villainy that
was perpetrated on that day in the neighbourhood.
In an adjoining precinct a Tillman champion
named Gaillard seized and destroyed the registration books, thus rendering the polling impossible
in default of duplicate books. Ballot-boxes, too,

are sometimes destroyed or made away with. Indeed, there is no conceivable scoundrelism that is not, or has not been, practised in the South to neutralise the negro vote.

From what I have written it will be clear that the extension of the suffrage to the coloured race in the Southern States by no means ensures the representation of the black man. The situation is a very disgraceful one for the Southern whites; but even the better class of Southern politicians with whom I have conversed upon the subject tacitly, if not expressly, defend, as with one voice, the iniquitous system. " We cannot," they say, " be ruled by the negroes; we must protect ourselves. It is very lamentable; but what is the alternative ? "

It is hard to suggest a practicable one, for the fatal and irretrievable mistake of bestowing the suffrage upon every male citizen of full age has already been made. That mistake is recognised as such not only by the Democrats, not only by the whites. Senator Ingalls, whom I have already spoken of as a Republican, wrote in the *North American Review*, in April, 1886 :—" Had the Republican party been courageous or intelligent enough to have attempted the reconstruction of the South through its brains rather than through its numbers, the most lamentable chapter in our

history might have been unwritten." And Mr.
A. M. E. Church, an intelligent coloured clergyman of Vicksburg, wrote, in the same year:—"We
will say . . . . that the mass of negroes
would do themselves and their country more good
if the ballot were out of their reach."

Congress has it in its power to limit the suffrage; but at this time of day it will not exercise
that power, which, by the way, ought never to
have been taken out of the hands of individual
States. The situation in Maine, where nearly all
the people are white and educated, is not like the
situation in Mississippi, where more than half the
people are black and ignorant. But Congress forgot that fact, and Amendment XV. took from the
States, practically for ever, a wholesome power,
which, under sec. 2, Art. 1, of the original Constitution, they had up to that moment been at
liberty to exercise. The repeal of Amendment
XV., however, would not settle, and would, in
my humble opinion, scarcely assist, the solution
of the race question. The cause of difficulty lies
far deeper; and this, I think, will appear when I
shall have considered the Southern negro in his
social and general, as well as in his political,
position, and when I shall have given some
examples of the force of race prejudice in
America.

Throughout the South the social position of the man in whose veins negro blood courses is unalterably fixed at birth. The child may grow to be wise, to be wealthy, to be entrusted even with the responsibilities of office, but he always bears with him the visible marks of his origin, and those marks condemn him to remain for ever at the bottom of the social ladder. To incur this condemnation he need not be by any means black. A quarter, an eighth, nay, a sixteenth of African blood, is sufficient to deprive him of all chances of social equality with the white man. For the being with the hated taint there is positively no social mercy. A white man may be ignorant, vicious, and poor. For him, in spite of all, the door is ever kept open. But the black, or coloured man, no matter what his personal merits may be, is ruthlessly shut out. The white absolutely declines to associate with him on equal terms. A line has been drawn; and he who, from either side, crosses that line has to pay the penalty. If it be the negro who dares to cross, cruelty and violence chase him promptly back again, or kill him for his temerity. If it be the white, ostracism is the recognised penalty. And it is not only the uneducated and the easily prejudiced who have drawn the line thus sharply. Speaking in 1858, Abraham Lincoln said :—

"I am not, and never have been, in favour of bringing about, in any form, the social and political equality of the white and the black races. There is a physical difference which forbids them from living together on terms of social and political equality. And, inasmuch as they cannot so live, while they do remain together there must be a position of superior and inferior, and I, as much as any other man, am in favour of having the superior position assigned to the whites."

Mr. Froude, in "The English in the West Indies," writes:—

"One does not grudge the black man his property, his freedom, his opportunity of advancing himself; one would wish him as free and prosperous as the fates and his own exertions can make him, with more and more means of raising himself to the white man's level. But left to himself, and without the white man to lead him, he can never reach it. . . . We have a population to deal with the majority of whom are an inferior race. Inferior, I am obliged to call them, because as yet they have shown no capacity to rise above the condition of their ancestors, except under European laws, European education, and European authority to keep them from war upon one another. . . . Give them independence, amd in a few generations they will peel off such civilisation as they have as easily and as willingly as their coats and trousers."

And, says Professor E. W. Gilliam, to whose writings on the subject I have already made some allusion:—

"The blacks have been, and must continue to be, a distinct and alien race; the fusion of races is the resultant from social equality and intermarriage, and the barrier to this is here insurmountable. The human species presents three grand varieties, marked off by colour—white, yellow, and black. One at the first, in origin and colour, the race multiplied and spread, and separate sections, settled in different latitudes, took on—under climatic conditions acting with abnormal force in that early and impressionable period of the race's age—took on, we say, different hues, which, as the race grew and hardened, crystallised into permanent characteristics. Social affinity exists among the families of these three groups. The groups themselves stand rigidly apart. The Irish, German, French, &c., who come to these shores readily intermarry among themselves and with the native population. Within a generation or two the sharpness of national feature disappears, and the issue is the American, whose mixed blood is the country's foremost hope. It cannot be—a fusion like this between blacks and whites. Account for it as we may, the antipathy is a palpable fact which no one fails to recognise —an antipathy not less strong among the Northern than among the Southern whites. However the former may, on the score of matters political, profess themselves special friends to the blacks, the question of intermarriage and social equality, when brought to practical test, they will not touch with the end of the little finger. Whether it be that the blacks, because of their former condition of servitude, are regarded as a permanently degraded class ; whether it be that the whites, from their historic eminence, are possessed with a consciousness of superiority which spurns alliance—the fact that fusion is impossible no one in his senses can deny."

Professor Gilliam wrote from a Southern standpoint, but, says Judge Albion W. Tourgée: " Looking at the subject from a standpoint diametrically opposed in every respect both to the intellectual bias and to the political inclination of Professor Gilliam, we are compelled to endorse his views in this respect almost without the least modification." And in another page of his admirable and informing volume, " An Appeal to Cæsar," Mr. Tourgée remarks, " When the freedman began to establish his own home circle, to build for himself a household about his own hearth, however humble, the distance between the whites and blacks, though in fact very greatly diminished, seemed to have been as greatly increased."

My own impression, as derived from somewhat wide observation, is that, since the emancipation, the distance has really as well as apparently increased, and that it is still increasing. Whites and blacks have less in common than of yore; there is less chance than there ever was of their working together peacefully for good; and racial antagonism, nourished by both sides, grows daily. There are many signs, too, of this growing antagonism. On the side of the negro there is a desire to be what the white man is, and to do what the white man does—to elevate himself to the same level of privileges, with or without the pre-requisite education and fitness for the elevation. He argues blindly that the legal right confers the needful fitness. The law opens positions to him, and he is a voter. Why then should he not vote himself and his friends into the positions? And education by no means tends to decrease the friction, seeing that the white man is as prejudiced against an educated negro as against an ignorant one. On the contrary, it adds to it. When the uneducated black thinks himself the equal of the white, the educated black cannot be expected to submit resignedly to be regarded as the white's inferior. Yet he is obliged to affect the resignation which he cannot feel. He must suppress his real sentiments, or he must risk physical maltreatment.

His social position cannot be properly understood without the aid of illustrations. I will therefore give a few, which are taken at hazard from some hundreds of examples that I might cite.

But, as an introduction to this branch of the subject, I must first quote a passage from Mr. George W. Cable's recent book, "The Silent South," a volume which is inspired from beginning to end with love—perhaps unwise love—for the negro, and with a desire to do all that lies in the writer's power to abate the prevalent race friction. Mr. Cable asks :—

"Are the freedman's liberties suffering any real abridgment? The answer is easy. The letter of the laws, with a few exceptions, recognises him as entitled to every right of an

American citizen; and to some it may seem unimportant that there is scarcely one public relation of life in the South where he is not arbitrarily and unlawfully compelled to hold toward the white man the attitude of an alien, a menial, and a probable reprobate, by reason of his race and colour. One of the marvels of future history will be that it was counted a small matter by a majority of our nation for six millions of people within it, made by its own decree a component part of it, to be subjected to a system of oppression so rank that nothing could make it seem small except the fact that they had already been ground under it for a century and a half. Examine it. It proffers to the freedman a certain security of life and property, and then holds the respect of the community, that dearest of earthly boons, beyond his attainment. It gives him certain guarantees against thieves and robbers, and then holds him under the unearned contumely of the mass of good men and women. It acknowledges in constitutions and statutes his title to an American's freedom and aspirations, and then in daily practice heaps upon him in every public place the most odious distinctions, without giving ear to the humblest plea concerning mental or moral character. It spurns his ambition, tramples upon his languishing self-respect, and indignantly refuses to let him either buy with money, or earn by any excellence of inner life or outward behaviour, the most momentary immunity from these public indignities even for his wife and daughters."

In America it is a matter of notoriety that there is no exaggeration here, nor is the race feeling confined solely to the South. To the British reader the following cases in point will, I believe, prove that there is no exaggeration :—

"Supposing the Courts of our Southern States, while changing no laws requiring the impanelling of jurymen without distinction as to race, &c., should suddenly begin to draw their thousands of jurymen all black, and well-nigh everyone of them counting not only himself, but all his race, better than any white man. Assuming that their average of intelligence and morals should be not below that of jurymen as now drawn, would a white man, for all that, choose to be tried in one of those Courts? Would he suspect nothing? Could one persuade him that his chances of even justice were all they should be, or all they would be, were the Court not evading the law in order to sustain an outrageous distinction against him because of the accident of his birth? Yet, only read white man for black man, and black man for white man, and that—I speak as an eye-witness—has been the practice for years, and is still so to-day ; an actual emasculation, in the case of six million people, both as plaintiff and defendant, of the right of trial by jury."— MR. G. W. CABLE.

"The negro children of the city are usually the aggressors when trouble occurs between them and white children. Both colours are too ready for a row, but coloured parents are too ready to teach their youngsters that white people are their natural enemies. We daily see negro boys trying all their ingenuity to get a fight out of the white boys when the latter try to avoid a row, and this is peculiarly true when there are two or three young negroes to one white. Negro girls are apt to be extremely insolent, not only to whites of their own age, but to ladies. In the matter of collisions between school-boys, that may best be left to the police. The negro girls who push white women and girls off the walks can be cured of that practice by the use of a horsewhip; and we advise white fathers and husbands to use the whip. It's a great corrective." —Chattanooga *Times.*

This advocacy of the summary horsewhipping of girls is very significant of the brutal attitude of the Southern white towards the negro.

"Between two and three o'clock an excursion train, composed entirely of coloured people, arrived at Gouldsboro depôt from Bâton Rouge. A large number of coloured men and women were near the depôt waiting for the train, which was due at eleven o'clock. As the train neared the depôt, one of the excursionists attempted to get off and fell to the ground. Some unknown person made a personal remark, when the negro drew a pistol and fired four or five shots in rapid succession, one of which struck a white man named William Miller, brother of one of the Gretna police, in the nose and lodged itself in the back of his neck. Then the shooting became general, some four or five hundred shots being fired in less than fifteen minutes. The stories of the blacks and whites as to the origin of the trouble differ widely. The negroes say that a large body of armed white men were awaiting the train's arrival, and that about ten minutes after it stopped they opened fire on the negroes who were going to the street car. The whites say that only half a dozen white men were concerned in the affair, and that the negroes, before the train came to a halt, fired two shots at a white boy named Burmester. Billy Miller was then shot by one of the white men, and then the fight became general."—Associated Press Telegram from New Orleans, September 1st, 1889.

"It is impossible for the negro to get any justice at the hands of Southern magistrates or juries. A man who resides in Augusta, Ga.—a Democrat and a hater of the negro—admits that the whites' maltreatment of the blacks must one day recoil upon their own heads. 'Why,' said he to me to-day, 'you can't convict a white man of the murder of a negro, nor even

of a white friend of the negro. Just before I left home a
negro was found one morning in the street, with his body
riddled with bullets. I was pretty certain that his death was
due to a certain gang of roughs, whose leader is under obliga-
tion to me for keeping him out of the penitentiary. Meeting
him I said, "Pat, who killed that nigger?" "Oh, some of the
boys," said Pat, with a grin. "What did they do it for?" I
asked. "Oh, because he was a nigger," said Pat. "And," he
continued, "he was the best nigger in town. Why, he would
even take off his hat to me."' I thought he must be a good
negro, indeed, who would take off his hat to that creature, and
I walked away pondering upon what must be the outcome of it
all. It is my opinion that several of the Southern States will
have to be abandoned to the negroes if we would avoid terrible
consequences from the wrongs we are heaping on them."
—Washington correspondence of the Pittsburg *Dispatch*,
January 11th, 1890.

"They had an election down in Jackson, Miss., yesterday,
and it was of the usual kind. The regular press reports, with
charming frankness, state that everything was progressing
quietly so long as the negroes stayed away from the polls; but
should the black men attempt to exercise the right of suffrage
there would be trouble."—Philadelphia *Evening Telegram*,
January 7th, 1890.

A negro named William Black stole some trifling articles
from the house of a white man, one Jim Bennett, near Robins,
South Carolina. Bennett followed and caught the negro, and,
assisted by Dave Ready, Henry Sweat, and John Walker, tied
the prisoner to a tree. Ready then placed a gun to the negro's
temple and blew out the man's brains. Bennett, Walker, and
Sweat were arrested as accessories in the first degree, but were
discharged by Justice Dunbar. Ready apparently escaped.—
Summarised from a Barnwell letter of January 11th, 1890, in
the Charleston *Budget*.

Two boys—Williams, a negro, and Robertson, a white—
were playing together near Waynesboro with a gun, which,
being accidentally discharged, killed Robertson. The negro boy
was arrested, but was taken from custody by a mob of white
men, who tied him up and shot him to death.—Summarised
from a despatch from Augusta, Georgia, dated October 24th,
1890, to the Charleston *News and Courier.*

"A Tennessee white man was hanged on Tuesday for the
brutal murder of his wife. The despatches tell us that he
objected to going on the gallows with three coloured men who
were to be hanged at the same time, and that the authorities so
far respected his prejudices as to swing off the negroes first."—
New York *Star*, January 7th, 1890.

"Some years ago a great revival was going on in one of the
churches of my own city. The evangelist was fervidly inviting
all kinds of people to come to the 'anxious seat.' Crowds of
men, women, and children were accepting the invitation.
Tramps, drunkards, and beggars were among the number. At
last it was announced to the church officials that a negro upon
one of the back seats was 'under conviction.' Here was a
problem of serious import. The officials held a hurried and
anxious consultation, and it was finally decided that the negro
might receive the benefit of salvation in an inconspicuous pew.
This case might fairly be termed exceptional if it were not true
that one of the largest and most influential denominations in
the land, having been split in half by the question of slavery,
remains in that condition to-day solely on the question of
colour caste."—Rev. JOHN SNYDER, in the *Forum*, October,
1889. (The denomination alluded to is the American Presbyterian Church.)

"While the Republican whoopers at the North are bursting
with indignation at the fact that the negroes on Southern rail-
roads are provided with separate cars from those occupied by
the whites, they have not a word of protest against the fact

that a daughter of a Southern negro ex-Governor was 'frozen' out of the ball-room of the Grand Union Hotel at Saratoga a few nights ago. The gathering in the ball-room was not of persons specially invited, but was made up, as such watering-place balls usually are, of the guests stopping in the hotel. The young lady in question is beautiful and accomplished, and above all moral reproach, and so slightly tinted with negro blood that she would have passed muster among whites almost anywhere in the matter of colour. In spite, however, of all the facts in her favour, the single circumstance of race created, in a crowded assemblage in a Northern State, a sentiment that immediately culminated in outward expressions which at once convinced the unfortunate lady that she was an object of most unfriendly observation on the part of the people gathered there."—New Orleans *Picayune*, August 30th, 1889.

"The report comes from South Carolina that a coloured man, unarmed and defenceless, fell into an altercation with a white man of that State named Gallman. Gallman slit the coloured man's throat from ear to ear, and drove to a neighbour's house, where he procured a shot-gun, and emptied the contents of one barrel into the wounded man. At a late hour that night Mr. Gallman's friends, hearing that the victim had not died, although he was at death's door, rode to where he lay, and carried him to the nearest churchyard, where they riddled his body with bullets."—Boston *Advertiser*, June 2nd, 1889.

"A reporter of the New York *World* on Saturday disguised himself as a wealthy negro from Cuba, and went around to the various first-class hotels to secure accommo-dation for himself. That must have been a busy day with the hotel people, for the clerks smilingly told him that every room was engaged. Seeing that it would be impossible to secure a room, he then tried to get something to eat. At most of the restaurants the waiters would pay no attention to his

H

orders, and the cashiers with one accord assured him that the proprietor was out and would not return until late. At the Hoffman House Café he was given food, but was not served at the bar. At Delmonico's he was assured that they had nothing to eat. So it seems that the prejudice against the negro is not confined entirely to the South."—New York *World*, June, 1888.

Last year Mr. Douglass, a mulatto, was appointed United States Minister to Hayti, and was taken thither on board an American man-of-war, the *Kearsage*. Another ship, the *Ossipee*, was first ordered to convey him. It is alleged that her commander, being unwilling to carry and associate with a coloured man, urged as an excuse that his vessel was not fit for sea. The officers of the *Kearsage* refused to dine with the Minister. "The army officers are in a state of glee over it, and so are the Navy officers on duty here. All unite in saying that if any of the *Kearsage* officers dine with Douglass on the way to Hayti they will find themselves tabooed by their brother officers thereafter."—Summarised from the Washington correspondence of the St. Louis *Republic*, October, 1889.

"We simply hate, as American citizens, to be told by our equals *de jure* 'Thus far shalt thou go, and no farther.' The blackest hands can cook the food for prejudiced throats; the blackest, dirtiest arms can hold the whitest, cleanest baby; the blackest, most illiterate man can sit on the same seat, even with a lady, as a driver; but the angry passions rise when a well-dressed, educated, refined negro pays his own fare and seats himself quietly in a public conveyance."—Orangeburg *Plain Speaker*, a negro newspaper, December 4th, 1889.

"Two coloured men, respectable in appearance and well educated, the one principal of, and the other a teacher in, a public school of the city, entered a restaurant in Cincinnati the other day. They seated themselves at a table, but no

waiter went near them, and when they finally asked to be
served they were thrown out into the street. The sole trouble
was the fact that they were coloured."—New York *Evening
Post*, December 31st, 1889.

" Social equality of whites and blacks is unheard of here,
even in 'black' Republican circles. The whites don't want it
and the blacks won't have it. Any white person who
advocates it here is quietly ignored as an irredeemable crank,
and the South can afford to keep cool and follow Northern
example regarding this deadest of dead issues."—New York
Herald, November, 1889.

" Wednesday will be long remembered in Georgia as the
day on which an unparalleled number of violent crimes were
committed. At Jessop a bloody riot occurred; at Augusta
there was a conflict approaching the dimensions of a riot,
accompanied by bloodshed. At Dainesville a very worthy
coloured man was, it appears, cruelly murdered ; at Toombsboro
another negro was killed ; and at Greeneville a shooting affair
occurred. . . . The quarrel was in every instance between
men of different colour."—Macon *Telegraph*, December 28th,
1889.

" A few days ago a negro minister of this city boarded the
east-bound passenger train on the E.T.V. and G. Railway, and
took a seat in the coach occupied by white passengers. Some
of the passengers complained to the conductor and brakemen,
and expressed considerable dissatisfaction that they were
forced to ride alongside of a negro. The railway officials
informed the complainants that they were not authorised to
force the coloured passenger into the coach set apart for the
negroes, and they would lay themselves liable should they do
so. The white passengers then took the matter in their own
hands, and ordered the ebony-hued minister to take a seat in
the next coach. He positively refused to obey orders, whereupon the white men gave him a sound flogging and forced him

H 2

to a seat among his own colour and equals. We learned yesterday that the vanquished preacher was unable to fill his pulpit on account of the severe chastisement inflicted upon him."—Selma (Alabama) *Times*, quoted by Mr. G. W. Cable.

" There is terrible excitement here over the co-education of the races. The Alton Board of Education has provided separate schools for coloured children, but the negroes want their children to attend the schools set apart for the whites. They had threatened and threatened to force their way into the schools and put their children alongside the whites, and flatly refused to permit their children to attend the school-houses set apart for the negro children. These threats, how-ever, until to-day, were looked upon as idle and meaningless. This morning the negroes took action in the matter. Scores of adult negroes, accompanied by half a hundred black children, went to the high school and demanded admission. Super-intendent Powell is a mild-mannered man, and offered no obstructions. The black children walked in and took posses-sion of all the desks they found unoccupied. The white pupils protested, and began to pick up their books and make preparations to leave. Some of the coloured boys grinned at the white girls, and as soon as the negro men left the building the white pupils assaulted the blacks. There was a hard fight for fifteen minutes, during which books, inkstands, rulers, slates and hair filled the air. The whites finally drove the blacks out of the room and chased them out of the yard, and continued to fight in the street. The white girls urged their champions on with encouraging shouts, and brought them munitions of war when possible."—General Press Telegram from Alton, Illinois, January 11th, 1890.

" At Decatur, Ill., Wood Bros., purveyors of candles and ice-cream, had no ice-cream to sell to the Rev. Edward Wilson. He was a negro. He now arrests the purveyors by virtue of the Civil Rights Law, and 'the case will be hotly contested.'

THE EX-SLAVE AS HE IS.

Of course it will. And the jury will discharge the confec-
tioners. The black man will get no ice-cream. The people of
Decatur love the negro in the South, not in the North. The
Civil Rights Bill was prepared for the South, where a coloured
man can get all the ice-cream he may pay for. To apply Reconstruction to the North—is not that oppressive? The same
Northerner who will endure arrest before he will sell ice-cream
to a black man will tell you confidently that the determination
of the Southerners to prevent black home rule is the vilest
conspiracy of modern times."—Chicago *Herald*, September 6th,
1889.

"One hot night in September. . . . I was travelling
by rail in the State of Alabama. At rather late bedtime there
came aboard the train a young mother and her little daughter
of three or four years. They were neatly and tastefully
dressed in cool, fresh muslins, and as the train went on its way
they sat together very still and quiet. At the next station
there came aboard a most melancholy and revolting company.
In filthy rags, with vile odours, and the clanking of shackles
and chains, nine penitentiary convicts chained to one chain,
and ten more chained to another, dragged laboriously into
the compartment of the car where in one corner sat this
mother and child, and packed it full, and the train moved
on. The keeper of the convicts told me he should take
them in that car 200 miles that night. They were going to
the mines. My seat was not in that car, and I stayed in
it but a moment. It stank insufferably. I returned to my
own place in the coach behind, where there was, and had
all the time been, plenty of room. But the mother and
child sat on in silence in that foul hole, the conductor having distinctly refused them admission elsewhere because they
were of African blood, and not because the mother was, but
because she was not, engaged at the moment in menial service.
Had the child been white, and the mother not its natural but

its hired guardian, she could have sat anywhere in the train."
—MR. G. W. CABLE.

" During a day's stay in Atlanta lately, the present
writer saw many things greatly to admire. . . . He feels
constrained to ask whether it must be that in the principal
depôt of such a city the hopeless excommunication of every
person of African tincture from the civil rewards of gentility
must be advertised by three signs at the entrances of three
separate rooms, one for 'Ladies,' one for 'Gentlemen,' and
the third a ' Coloured Waiting-room ?' Visiting the principal
library of the city, he was eagerly assured, in response to
inquiry, that no person of colour would be allowed to draw out
books."—MR. G. W. CABLE.

" Postmaster Lewis and Colonel A. E. Buck were hung in
effigy in front of the Court-house to-night, in the presence of
probably 10,000 persons. This action was the result of Lewis
appointing a negro to a place in the Registry Department,
where he would come in contact with a white lady clerk."—
Letter from Atlanta, Georgia, of August 8th, 1889, to Charleston *News and Courier.*

" The Rev. J. Francis Robinson, a Baptist preacher of
good character, has been visiting in the City of Auburn, New
York. The day after his arrival he wished to get shaved, and
went to a barber-shop, but was refused attention. He went
in succession to several other barber-shops, but received the
same treatment at each. The Rev. F. D. Penny, pastor of
the Second Baptist Church in Auburn, accompanied the Rev.
Mr. Robinson to a number of shops, and offered the proprietors
a dollar to shave his friend, but his co-operation was of no use.
The trouble was that the Rev. Mr. Robinson had a black skin,
and, as one of the barbers said, 'I refused to shave him
because it is against the rules of the trade to shave a coloured
man.' "—New York *Evening Post*, August 6th, 1889.

" Deacon J. H. Brown, of the First African Baptist

Church, of this city, had quite an unpleasant experience at
Baxley yesterday. He is on his way, along with other
coloured deacons and clergymen, to a convention of the church
at Indianapolis. Six of them entered the white people's
coach, filled largely with ladies, and, despite the repeated
protests of the passengers, would not vacate their seats. One
passenger wired to Baxley over the signature of ' Passenger,'
asking for help to put the negroes out, and stating that he
would make himself known when the train arrived. When
Baxley was reached a crowd of men boarded the train and
requested the negroes to leave. They refused. This did not
change their purpose, and force was then used. In the fight
that ensued two men were cut, but not very seriously. The
train pulled out quickly to prevent further disturbance, and a
physician at Lumber City was telegraphed for to meet the
wounded men there. He refused, but subsequently one was
secured and the men cared for. Brown was hurt about the
head and face from blows inflicted by a club."—Savannah
(Georgia) *Times,* September 10th, 1889.

"The colour line question has nearly caused a split in the
Independent Baptists' Union. An organisation composed of
Baptist ministers of Virginia, West Virginia, and Maryland
is in session here. The Rev. H. A. Braxton, a coloured
member, objected to the use of the word ' coloured ' in a
report referring to work among his race. This objection fired
the Southern sentiment of some of the white brethren, and a
sharp discussion ensued. Preacher Braxton declared that he
was opposed to ecclesiastical bossism, and wanted the colour
line buried. Dr. A. C. Dickinson, editor of the *Religious
Herald,* of Richmond, asked : ' Do you want us to treat you
every way as if you were not coloured ? ' The Rev. Mr. Braxton
replied : ' Yes, we want to be treated as men, and we want
no special favours.' The Rev. A. C. Dickinson said : ' Do
you want us to bury the colour line ? If so, where is it to be

buried—on the white side or on the black? The colour is
there. God put it there. Leaving out the word " coloured"
won't help it. Now, what are you going to do about it? Do
you intend to give up your convention and your churches and
join ours, or do you want us to give up ours and join yours?'
Rev. Dr. J. W. M. Williams, one of the most prominent
Baptists in the South, said: 'If you (the coloured people)
don't intend to stop talking on this question, then, in the name
of the Lord, go by yourselves and talk all day on the question
of colour. If the coloured people see they can do their work
better alone, let them go and work by themselves.'"—General
Press Telegram from Baltimore, Maryland, October 18th, 1889.

"A delegation of citizens waited on Governor Gordon
to-day, and asked him to take action concerning the whipping
of a number of negroes by unknown white men at East Point,
near Atlanta. The affair occurred late last night. It was
the outgrowth of the lynching of a negro boy on Wednesday
night for the usual crime. The negroes had a mass meeting,
and the citizens, becoming alarmed, sent for police from Atlanta.
The presence of the officers prevented further trouble, but
after they had gone a number of white men went to different
cabins and whipped the negroes, fourteen in all."—Atlanta
despatch of September 6, 1889, to Charleston *News and
Courier.*

A man named L. P. Smith was employed as a detective.
He arrested one Jackson, a negro, mistaking him for a
murderer who was "wanted." Finding out his error, but
desiring to secure the reward, he offered to release Jackson if
the latter would submit to have one of his ears cut off, that
ear bearing a mark similar to one on the ear of the sought-for
murderer. Jackson agreed. Smith, uneasy as to what he
had done, then shot Jackson, who, however, lived long enough
to make a statement.—Summarised from a Birmingham
(Alabama) despatch of September, 1889.

The mutilated bodies of Rosmond Cormier, coloured, and his daughter Rosalie were found in a cabin on the Abbeville Road, near Lafayette, Louisiana. Cormier, who was sixty, had been previously whipped and ordered by a band of " Regulators" to leave the district, but had not complied. The " Regulators " returned, demanded admittance to the cabin, were refused, and were fired at in self-defence by Cormier. They then shot him and cut his daughter's throat from ear to ear. On the same night they very severely whipped two other negroes.— Summarised from a New Orleans despatch of September 11th, 1889, to the Charleston *News and Courier.*

" In Fulton County, Georgia, a black boy of eighteen years was taken from gaol and hanged for ' assaulting ' a white girl, the assault consisting of catching the child by the arms and running away when she and her companion screamed. Then a pack of white ruffians, heavily armed, went from one cabin to another in an alleged search for a criminal, and barbarously whipped and maltreated inoffensive negroes, who were powerless to defend themselves against shot-guns and revolvers presented at their heads."—*Greenville News,* September 10th, 1889.

" There are symptoms of a race war in Missouri, at Dexter. . . . The people in that section have for years excluded all negroes from among them. A short time ago a man named Williams settled on a farm there, and engaged a dozen negroes to work for him. Fifty armed white men waited upon him this week, and told him he must get rid of the negroes. He said they might kill him first. The armed men returned to town, where they are circulating a paper pledging the signers to stand by the 'Regulators.'"—*Charleston News and Courier,* September 14th, 1889.

" Robert Battey, a negro juror, was refused admission to the dining-room at the Augusta Hotel yesterday. He was the only coloured man on the jury, which was empanelled to try a criminal case in the City Court, and when the hour of dinner arrived the case was of such importance that Judge Eve ordered the jury to be kept together. . . . Upon arriving at the hotel Mr. B. S. Doolittle, the proprietor, who is, by the way, a Northern man, refused Battey, the coloured juror, admission to his dining-room, where a number of ladies and gentlemen were seated at dinner. Mr. Doolittle offered to furnish the coloured juror with his meal in another room, but Battey would not consent to be isolated in that manner, and before he would go into the private room he went home, where he enjoyed his usual meal in custody of an officer. This attempted intrusion of a negro into the dining-hall of an hotel called forth considerable comment, and Mr. Doolittle was upheld in his refusal to serve Battey with dinner at the same table with white people."—Augusta (Georgia) despatch of October 4th, 1889, to Charleston *News and Courier.*

I have, perhaps, cited sufficient examples of white intolerance and tyranny. These character-istics are, it will have been observed, not exclus-ively confined to the South. I should add that, in several States, what is known as miscegenation, or, to be plain, marriage between a white and a black or coloured person, is illegal.

After reading what I have written and quoted, can any one fail to ask himself these questions? Is there any doubt that there is a race problem of infinite difficulty and danger awaiting, nay crying for, solution in America? Is it not true that there is practically one law for the black and

another for the white in the South? Is it likely
that the negro's civil rights will ever be respected
by the Southern whites? Can civilisation admit
the claim of the South to be permitted to settle
the race question in its own way? Is it not the
duty of the United States to deal with the question? Is the position of the Southern black likely
to become more tolerable or less, under the existing
system? I might insist much more than I have
done upon the negro's unfortunate situation. I
might picture him, in all detail, as he is in the
school, in the church, and even in the graveyard
—a being kept remorselessly apart from his white
fellows. But I am anxious not to be one-sided,
and not to allow my natural sympathy for the
black man's wrongs to render me blind to the fact
that the white man, too, has wrongs great and intolerable. What these wrongs are I shall attempt
to show when I deal with the position of the
Southern white. In the meanwhile I will conclude my present division of the subject with a
few notes on the sanitary, moral, educational, and
material position of the Southern negro of to-day.

As to his sanitary position I have, I regret
to say, no very modern statistics at my disposal. The latest that convey a fairly broad
view of the situation apply to the years 1883
and 1885; but there is no doubt that things

have very little changed since then. The death-rate, among children under five years old, per 1,000 of the whole population, for the year 1883 was—in Charleston, white 5·88, coloured 21·3; in Memphis, white 3·75, coloured 13·91; in Nashville, white 5·65, coloured 12·44; and in Savannah, white 7·59, coloured 18·01. The rate in 1885 was—in Charleston, white 4·45, coloured 14·38; in Memphis, white 4·67, coloured 13·46; in Nashville, white 4·37, coloured 10·78; and in Savannah, white 4·23, coloured 13·70. Squalid dwellings, in filthy neighbourhoods, impure air, dirty water, neglect of personal cleanliness, immorality, extensive meat consumption without vegetable diet to match, and gregarious and generally unsavoury habits, induce a black mortality which, at least in the large centres, is enormous, and is particularly noticeable under the heads of consumption, pneumonia, and scrofula.

Bearing upon this point, a paragraph from the New York *Tribune*, of August 20th, 1889, deserves quotation :—

"As the result of extended observations, including thousands of cases, thirty-six per cent. being negroes and mulattoes, Dr. L. McLane Tiffany, of Baltimore, finds some marked differences in the diseases of whites and blacks. Thus, spinal caries is more frequently located in the dorsal region of the negro, and a cured case of Pott's disease in the middle-

aged negro is very rare ; dislocations are more frequent in the
white, as is also lateral curvature of the spine ; keloid is
characteristically more frequent in the negro, likewise lipoma.
Although Dr. Tiffany has never seen an epithelioma of the lip or
any part of the face in a negro, osteo-sarcoma is often met
with in the race. In hospital cases, the negro bears operations
better, as a rule, than the white, but their reaction after
accidents is not so good as that of the latter. Dr. Tiffany
concludes that surgical affections pursue different courses in
the white and coloured races under identical hygienic
surroundings ; that surgical diseases involving the lymphatic
system, especially tubercular, are more fatal in negroes than in
whites ; that congenital deformities are more rare in negroes
than in whites ; and that surgical differences observed between
negroes and whites are due to racial peculiarities."

Yet the excess of mortality among the coloured
people, large though it be, is more than counter-
balanced by their superior fecundity. This is
very remarkable, seeing that in many cities where
the whites outnumber the blacks as two to one,
the death-rate among the latter positively exceeds
that among the former. In Charleston, for example, the death-rate in 1884 was for the whites
1 in 42, and for the coloured 1 in 22 ; and in
1883, for the whites 1 in 46, and for the coloured 1
in 21. This is rendered the more striking by the
fact that the poorer coloured people in Charleston
are supplied with medicines and medical attention at the expense of the city. In 1884 no fewer
than 17,950 coloured patients were treated in the

city hospital and in the different health districts, as against only about one-third of that number of white patients.   In 1886 the Charleston death-rate was, per 1,000, for whites 20·65 and for coloured 49·01.   In 1887, out of 41,000 whites in Atlanta, Georgia, 608 died, while out of 22,000 coloured people 707 died.   Again, in the week ending March 9, 1889, the estimated population of New Orleans was—whites, 184,500; coloured, 69,500; and the death-rate per 1,000 was—whites, 14·13; coloured, 30·03. . And the story is much the same everywhere.   The negroes die like flies, and increase only because they also breed like flies.

Their moral condition, as shown by criminal statistics and by the testimony of competent observers, is equally unsatisfactory.   Says the Rev. Dr. Tucker, formerly of Jackson, Mississippi :—

" In all the country districts the removal of the restraints of slavery, such as they were, has resulted in an open abandonment of every semblance of morality and the loss almost of the idea of marriage.   Why, in one county of Mississippi, there were during twelve months 300 marriage licences taken out in the county clerk's office for white people.   According to the proportion of population, there should have been in the same time 1,200 or more for negroes.   There can be no legal marriage of any sort in Mississippi without a licence.   There were actually taken out by coloured people just three ! . . .   Soon after the war the Legislature passed an Act legalising the

union of all who were then living together, marrying them
whether they wished or not ; and for years afterwards the
courts were crowded with applications for divorce from
coloured people, which mostly had to be granted, since there
was ample cause for divorce under either the Divine or the
statute law. I know of whole neighbourhoods, including
hundreds of negro families, where there is not one single
legally married couple, or couple not married, who stay
faithful to each other beyond a few months, or a few years at
most; often but a few weeks. And if out of every 500 negro
families one excepts a few dozen who are legally married, this
statement will hold true for millions of coloured people. And
these things I tell you to-night are but hints. I cannot, I
dare not, tell the full truth before a mixed audience."

These words were originally spoken before
the Episcopal Congress at Richmond, Virginia, in
1882; they were subsequently published in a
pamphlet, and I am generally assured, and im-
plicitly believe, that they were true then and are
true now. Even the negroes themselves dare not
deny them. One negro preacher published a
pamphlet, in which he admitted that—

"This speech reveals humiliating facts, so truthful, yet
hard to acknowledge. Not one of our social circles, if we can
be said to have any, is clean morally. They are full of base,
downright hypocrisy and falsehood, and full two-thirds of the
whole are members of the churches. Moral character is not
the standard. Crimes that should cause a blush on fair cheeks
assume a front of brass, and defy you to speak of or talk
about them. . . . A coloured man, only a few days ago,

contended with me that the negroes were right in certain of their practices, because the Lord Jesus himself said that 'Seven women should lay hold of one man.' "

Such was the confession of the Rev. Isaac Williams, with whom four other negro preachers fully concurred, adding—

"Our acquaintance extends over seven to ten thousand coloured people, concerning whose lives we know the truth, and that truth is set forth in Dr. Tucker's speech without exaggeration. There are exceptions, but the general truth is stated exactly as it is. We agree also that he has only given hints as regards many things of such a nature that only hints are possible."

On this repulsive subject I also have said enough. Nor will I say much concerning the degrading superstitions and superstitious practices of the great mass of ignorant blacks. Two years ago the *Herald*, a respectable paper in Boston, published an article five and a half columns long, the object of which was to demonstrate that Voodooism existed to an alarming extent among the coloured people of Boston and New England generally. Here are a couple of extracts:—

"No people are so prone by nature and force of circumstances to superstition as the blacks. Devout and easily excited, they are apt to accept, blindly and without reasoning, the traditions of their fathers; and even among those of reasonable education there are traces of the idolatrous creeds and customs which have always characterised the West India

Negroes. Voodooism, of which much has been hinted, a little written, but almost nothing known—one of the blackest, cruelest, and most heathenish forms of idolatry the world has ever seen—exists to-day to an alarming extent right here in Puritan New England."

"Perhaps the fact that the negroes have always regarded themselves as a wronged people impels them to cultivate a revengeful spirit ; and the prevailing object of their so-called spells is in the direction of working harm to their enemies. They pay more attention to vengeance than to the cure of diseases, although claiming wonderful power from their herbs and decoctions. The prevailing sentiment, if it may be so termed, of Voodooism, aside from idolatry, is revenge, and in their hatreds these people are implacable. No punishment is too horrible to be visited upon their enemies."

Most white Bostonians believed that the article was full of exaggerations, but, to the general surprise, the negroes practically admitted the impeachment.

Here is part of a resolution which was passed in July, 1889, by the Coloured National League sitting at Boston :—

"Whereas the Boston *Herald* has lately shown that the degrading superstition of Voodooism, as well as its practice, exists here in Boston to some extent among a few illiterate and ignorant persons of our race ; and whereas the sentiment among the better class of coloured people is that no one should be swifter to condemn any kind of foolish race superstition or disreputable practice than the coloured people themselves ; and whereas it should everywhere be the aim and desire of the coloured people to welcome any information that may show the

I

need of greater race enlightenment, or that shall stir us up to more earnest efforts for the general elevation of our people; be it resolved that the League places itself on record as being both anxious and willing to strike hands with the *Herald*, or any one else, in condemning, discountenancing, and stamping out Voodooism or any other 'ism' hurtful to the physical, moral, or spiritual elevation of the coloured people; and that the League calls upon good coloured people everywhere to set their face like a flint against every kind of evil superstition, habit, practice, custom, or belief, whose tendency, if encouraged, might be to degrade, belittle, or harm the coloured people in public estimation."

I may add that, not perhaps at Boston, but certainly in the South, and especially in Louisiana, Voodooism exists to-day. I pass on to criminal statistics as they concern the negro.

I will first take some suggestive statistics concerning the State of Mississippi, one of the " blackest " States in the Union, the population, according to the Census of 1880, having been —white, 479,398; coloured, 650,291. In the State Penitentiary on December 1, 1885, there were 103 white and 676 coloured males. Of the coloured people 113 were mulattoes, and the total number of coloured criminals in Mississippi in 1885 would be still further augmented if the number of judicial and irregular executions could be ascertained. As it is, it is clear that an unduly large proportion of criminality is furnished by the negro and negroid

population. Mr. H. S. Fulkerson, who has written
an interesting pamphlet on " The Negro " (Vicksburg, Mississippi, 1887), was induced by these
startling figures to go further into the subject, and
to examine the gaol register of Vicksburg, Mississippi, from March 1st, 1886, to February 28th,
1887. He found the commitments for the year to
have been 446, as many as 426 of the prisoners
being coloured, and only 20 white. The population
of Vicksburg in 1880 was—whites 5,975; coloured,
5,836. He also examined, for the same period,
the register of Vicksburg Workhouse, an institution in which violators of the city ordinances, &c.,
are confined. Of 1,416 persons committed 992
were coloured and 424 white. In 1889, in Charleston, 2,202 coloured persons were arrested, as
against only 1,250 whites. Most of the arrests during the year were made for the following offences :

	Whites.	Coloured.
Disorderly conduct	160	518
Drunk	248	165
Drunk and disorderly	242	291
Total	650	974

And here, to put the matter in a nutshell, are the
relative proportions, as gathered from the United
States Census of Prisoners, of black to white
criminality in half a dozen States:—Massachu-
I 2

setts, $2\frac{3}{4}$ to 1; Indiana, $6\frac{1}{4}$ to 1; Illinois, 2·4 to 1; Tennessee, 5 to 1; South Carolina, $6\frac{3}{4}$ to 1; and Georgia, 7·8 to 1. Thus in Tennessee the coloured man is five times as prone to criminality as the white, and in Georgia nearly eight times. And it must be borne in mind that these figures deal only with that portion of the total criminality which finds its way into prison. They do not, and no official figures can, take into account the criminality which is summarily punished by the operation of lynch law; and every one who knows the South knows also that, out of every fifty persons who are lynched there, at least forty-nine are of coloured complexion. Of lynching, however, I shall speak later, for it is mainly reserved as a punishment for one particular crime, the prevalence of which has a most important bearing upon the position of the Southern white.

Educationally, the coloured man has undoubtedly made great progress since his emancipation. In the slavery days ignorance was imposed by law upon the slave. Says the South Carolinian statute of 1834 :—" If any person shall hereafter teach any slave to read or write, or procure any slave to be taught to read or write, such person, if a free white person, shall be fined not exceeding one hundred dollars for each offence and imprisonment not less than six months; or, if a free person of colour, shall be whipped not exceeding fifty lashes and fined not exceeding fifty dollars; and, if a slave, shall be whipped at the discretion of the Court not exceeding fifty lashes; the informer to be entitled to one half the fine and to be a competent witness." And up to the day of emancipation the slave was, with scarcely an exception, kept in the densest ignorance. From the close of the war to the taking of the tenth census only fifteen years elapsed. In that period the adult negro had not greatly advanced, but the negro youth had made an amount of progress which, though by no means startling, was, I think, distinctly encouraging. The following table shows (1) the illiteracy of the male adult negro, and (2) the illiteracy of the whole negro population of the Black Belt in 1880 :—

	Total Coloured Male Adults.	Illiterate Coloured Male Adults.	Total Coloured Population.	Total Coloured Illiterates.
Virginia	128,257	100,210	631,707	315,660
North Carolina	105,018	80,282	532,505	271,943
South Carolina	118,889	93,010	604,472	310,071
Georgia	143.471	116,516	725,274	391,482
Florida	27,489	19,110	126,838	60,420
Alabama	118,423	96,408	600,320	321,680
Mississippi	130,278	99,068	652,199	319,753
Louisiana	107,977	86,555	484,992	259,429
	879,802	691,159	4,358,357	2,250,438

Thus, while the proportion of male adults who could read and write was, roughly speaking, only one in four, the proportion of coloured people of all ages was one in two. I have been informed at Washington that the eleventh census is likely to show that in these States seven coloured people out of every ten have escaped the imputation of illiteracy; but at the same time I have been warned that " writing " necessarily implies nothing more than ability to laboriously trace a signature, and that "reading" does not involve the ability to mark, learn, and inwardly digest anything more abstruse than a sentence in monosyllables. As Judge Tourgée has said :—

"One of the encouraging phases of the present situation is the fact that a coloured man is proud of the distinction of being able to read and write. It is to him a sort of patent of nobility. It shows to the world that he has gone above the level, that he has come up above the mass of his fellows, and is worthy of distinction and consideration in this respect if in no other. Because of these facts the statistics of illiteracy among the coloured people are peculiarly unreliable."

We may accept them as such, and yet regard them as encouraging. The level of education is rising. It has not risen high, and the number of negroes who possess such an education as is the property of a senior boy at a London Board School may probably, even now, not mount to

six figures. But there is promise in the fact that
the race supplies for its own improvement over
16,000 school teachers. An educated negro has
supplied some statistics on the subject of coloured
education in the South :—

"In 1887-88," he writes, "there were 15,000 public schools,
having 1,118,556 pupils ; 16 normal schools, 119 teachers and
3,924 pupils, with property valued at $992,350 ; 31 schools for
secondary instruction, 247 teachers, with 6,555 students, and
property valued at $843,100 ; 11 colleges of arts and sciences,
79 teachers, 922 students, and property valued at $1,443,000 ;
two schools of science, 29 teachers, 840 students, and property
valued at $50,000 ; 16 theological schools, 77 teachers, 833
students, and $489,500 in property ; 4 law schools, 16 teachers,
81 students, and $40,000 in property ; 3 schools of medicine,
48 teachers, 165 students, and $80,000 in property ; while
there were 2,081 pupils in schools for the blind and dumb,
making a total of 16,430 teachers, 1,139,904 pupils, and
$3,934,950 in school property."

Unfortunately there are no symptoms whatever
that the spread of education among the negroes
is causing, or ever will cause, the diminution of
white prejudice against the race.

Concerning the material position of the negroes
opinions vary greatly. There is no doubt, however, that they are gradually acquiring property,
and, in a few cases, accumulating capital. It
was recently declared that coloured people owned
a million acres of land in Texas alone, paying

taxes there on twenty million dollars' worth of property, and there were in the State twenty-five coloured lawyers, one hundred coloured merchants, five thousand coloured mechanics, and fifteen newspapers conducted by coloured people. Somewhat similar statements have been made, by negro speakers and writers chiefly, concerning the progress of the race elsewhere. Says one journal :—

"Georgia's coloured people are making a good record for thrift and industry. In 1879 their property was valued at $5,182,398 ; but in 1887 the valuation was $8,939,479, showing a gain of 72½ per cent. during the nine years. In the same time the valuation of white men's property had risen from $229,777,150 to $332,565,442, a gain of only 44·6 per cent. approximately. These figures simply prove what the intelligent representatives of the negro race have said about the progress made, and go to illustrate anew that the negroes are working out their own future. The richest coloured woman in the South, Mrs. Amanda Ewas, who has a snug fortune of $400,000, lives in Atlanta."

On the other hand, the Charleston *News and Courier* points out that in Charleston the negroes stand just where they did in 1860 ; that the value of the property held by them to-day is just about the same as that held by the free negroes twenty-eight years ago, and that, strange to say, the coloured property-holders are of the same class as in 1860, namely, the descendants of negroes who were free before the war.

I have had an opportunity of examining the assessment rolls of Chatham County, in which the city of Savannah, Georgia, is situated. These, as compiled in the summer of 1889, give the following results :—

	Population.	Property.	Property per Head.
Whites	17,494	$126,420,780	$1,510
Coloured	27,515	571,450	21

The negroes and coloured people, therefore, who constitute 61 per cent. of the local population, hold only 2 per cent. of the local wealth.

On the same subject the New Orleans *Times-Democrat* says :—

" We doubt whether the value of property held by coloured men in New Orleans is any greater to-day than that held by the freedmen of colour in 1860, and yet both in New Orleans and throughout Louisiana the negro has been improving his condition steadily. It takes more than one generation, however, to raise a race held in bonds of slavery to the condition of property-holders. When the hundreds of millions of dollars that have been paid the negroes in wages and the millions wasted by them in the veriest trash are considered, it seems strange that so few dollars have been invested in land, houses, or any permanent property. The freedmen of colour who inherited land or houses have held on to them, or at least to a portion of them. The negroes engaged in any very profitable trade or business may have laid aside something and own some little property, but the great majority of the race, who are simply farm hands, labourers, or domestic servants, have acquired no permanent property of any kind."

As a further illustration of the relative status of blacks and whites in what may be regarded as a representative section of the Black Belt, I append some interesting and detailed official statistics of Richmond County, Georgia, a county which had a total population in 1870 of 25,724, and in 1880 of 34,665, and which is one of the most populous and well-to-do counties in the State. In it, moreover, the races are almost equally divided.

Polls for 1889—White 5,069, coloured 4,029; total 9,098. Polls for 1888—White 4,923, coloured 3,844; total 8,767—an increase of 331.

Lawyers in 1889—White 50, coloured 1; total 51. Lawyers in 1888—White 48, coloured 1; total 49—an increase of 2.

Doctors in 1889—White 53, coloured 1. In 1888—White 46, coloured 2—an increase of 6.

Dentists in 1889—White 11, coloured 1; and the same for 1888.

Acres of land owned in 1889—White 180,332, coloured 4,943; total 185,275. Acres in 1888—White 180,835¼, coloured 4,661; total 185,496¼—a decrease of 221¼ acres.

Aggregate value of land in 1889—White $1,571,550, coloured

$64,440; total $1,638,990. In 1888—White $1,619,720, coloured $66,810; total $1,686,530—a decrease of $47,540.

Aggregate value of city or town property in 1889—White $9,713,140, coloured $438,940; total $10,152,080. In 1888— white $9,364,150, coloured $416,620; total $9,980,770—an increase of $371,310.

The number of shares in State or national banks is the same for 1888 and 1889, and is 20,300, and they are all owned by the whites.

The value of shares of such bank stock for 1889 is returned at $887,000, and for 1888 was returned at $1,002,000, showing a decrease of $115,000.

Property owned by gas or electric light companies is all owned by whites, and is valued in 1889 at $203,840, and for 1888 was returned at $215,250, showing a decrease of $11,410.

Amount of money and solvent debts, notes, accounts, etc., for 1889—whites $1,358,890, coloured $150; total $1,359,040. In 1888—whites $1,491,630, coloured $150; total $1,491,780 —a decrease of $132,740.

Merchandise of every sort for 1889—whites $1,260,550, coloured $5,730; total $1,266,280. In 1888—whites $1,278,290, coloured $5,680; total $1,283,970—a decrease of $17,690.

The capital invested in shipping and tonnage is all white, and for 1889 is $16,200. In 1888 it was $27,620—a decrease of $11,420.

Stocks and bonds are all white, and for 1889 are returned at $1,209,120, and for 1888 at $1,400,630, showing a decrease of $191,510.

Cotton manufactories are all white, and are returned for 1889 at $4,023,300, against $3,946,000 for 1888—an increase of $77,300.

Iron works, foundries, etc., are all white, and are returned for 1889 at $33,500, against $35,500, showing a decrease of $2,000.

Value of household and kitchen furniture, pianos, organs, etc., for 1889—White $570,690, coloured $17,990 ; total $588,680. In 1888—White $550,300, coloured $14,490 ; total $564,790—an increase of $23,890.

Watches, silver plate, and jewellery for 1880—White $74,020, coloured $50 ; total $74,070. In 1888—White $77,950, coloured $50 ; total $78,000—a decrease of $3,930.

Horses, mules, hogs, sheep, cattle, etc., for 1889—White $200,140, coloured $12,820 ; total $212,960. In 1888— White $199,430, coloured $13,580 ; total $213,016—a decrease of $50.

Plantation and mechanical tools, law or other library books, pictures, etc., are all returned by whites, and for 1889 are $63,100, against $71,650 for 1888, showing a decrease of $8,550.

Cotton, corn, crops, and provisions held for sale on April 1st are all white, and are returned for $350 in 1889 and $2,000 in 1888, showing a decrease of $1,650.

Value of all other property not before enumerated for 1889—White $405,170, coloured $4,440 ; total $409,610. In 1888—White $343,430, coloured $3,960 ; total $357,390—an increase of $52,220.

Aggregate value of whole property in 1889—White $21,590,560, coloured $547,560 ; total $22,138,120. In 1888 —White $21,635,550, coloured $521,340; total $22,156,890 —an aggregated decrease of $18,770.

In view of facts like these, it is hard to know what to make of the favourite negro declaration that the coloured people will, in the not distant future, be as powerful in the South in the matter

of wealth as they already are in the matter of
numbers. I believe, nevertheless, that it may
be accepted that the material improvement in
the coloured man's condition is more noticeable
than his improvement in any other direction.
He lives more comfortably and dresses better
than he did eight or ten years ago ; and, as his
main ambitions are physical and material rather
than intellectual and æsthetic, he is entitled to
congratulate himself.

The general progress of the negro does not,
however, satisfy those who once cherished the
highest hopes on his behalf. Here is a suggestive,
and, as I happen to know, a true paragraph,
dated Atlanta, Georgia, June 1, 1889, which I
clip from a Southern newspaper :—

"A celebrated English philanthropist was buried here
yesterday, having died at the residence of his daughter, Mrs.
Booth. John Glazebrook was his name, and he was a citizen
of Manchester, England. He was a man of great wealth, and
becoming interested in the abolition of slavery in the United
States, spent thousands of pounds in aiding the agitation. He
paid the expenses of lecturers, had runaway slaves exhibited
before English audiences, and placed his fortune in the scales
to accomplish the abolition of human servitude. A few
months ago he decided to visit this country for the purpose
of seeing whether the negro had improved. He died with the
declaration that he had wasted his money, and that freedom
had brought no benefit to the negro."

CHAPTER IV.

IN the Southern States, and especially in the States which constitute the Black Belt, the Race Question has in recent years assumed far more serious proportions than is generally supposed. It has, in fact, assumed the proportions of a species of guerilla race war. Few people, even in America, thoroughly realise this. The leading newspapers of the country pay surprisingly little attention to occurrences outside the district in which they find the majority of their readers. There is, so far as I am aware, no neutral journal which busies itself exclusively with the problem, and, consequently, Americans and foreigners alike are without any mirror in which they may periodically see reflected all the aspects and all the incidents of the situation. To keep up with the history of the Race Question the student must read, not the great newspapers of New York, Philadelphia, Boston, Chicago, or New

Orleans, but rather the little county newspapers of the South—newspapers the very names of which are scarcely known in the North and wholly unknown in Europe. And even these rural newspapers must be read with discretion and discrimination, for all of them are partisans. Some make a point of dwelling at length upon accounts of outrages committed by negroes, and of almost ignoring accounts of outrages committed by whites; others—they are, it is true, in the minority—follow the opposite plan. A few only are fair; a few only would care to print so free a confession as the following, which I take from the Augusta (Georgia) *Chronicle*, of Jan. 5th, 1890 :—

"Laws are powerless either to prevent the commission of crime or to punish criminals, unless public sentiment forbids the one and commands the other. Where there is little regard for human life, and we fear this is the case in many portions of our country, the courts are often to blame for not hanging those who slay their fellow-men. Is it not a fact that it is almost impossible to convict a man of the crime of murder who has any social position or means to defend himself? Fortunately, crimes of this sort do not often occur; but, if they did, public sentiment is so demoralised that the courts would fail of conviction. This is true as to white men who kill their equals. If a negro kills a white man, he is pretty sure either to be lynched or hung. But if a white man slays a negro, he is in no danger of being lynched, and as to his being hung for the crime there is not much probability."

To understand, therefore, both sides of the question, and to fully appreciate the seriousness of the situation, one must be a far more omnivorous devourer of newspapers than the ordinary citizen of Great Britain or of America has time to be. I have had exceptional opportunities. While I was in the country I met the leading men of both sides, and had thrust upon me the newspapers, big and little, of both parties. Nay, many people who for years have made a study of the subject were so good as to place their notes and their volumes of illustrative newspaper clippings at my disposal. Thus I may pretend to have secured the broadest and most far-reaching view of the difficulties amid which the South stands; and I cannot hide from myself the conclusion that, as between the races, the situation throughout the Black Belt is veritably, as I have said, one of active though unprofessed guerilla warfare. In the last chapter I gave a number of examples, selected almost at hazard from a far larger number which I might have cited, of the manner in which this warfare is being waged by the whites against the blacks. In this I shall give examples, similarly selected to a great extent, of the manner in which this warfare is being waged by the blacks against the whites. I have, I think, amply demonstrated the existence

J

of hostility on the white side. What I shall
quote now may, in the opinion of many, provide
good excuse for the existence of that hostility;
but I would submit that it also proves the
inherent and unconquerable mutual antipathy of
the races and their hopeless unsuitability for life
side by side and upon a level of approximate
equality. The antipathy is not between individual blacks and whites. It is rather such an
antipathy as used to exist between Turks and
Slavs in the Balkan provinces in the days of the
Bulgarian atrocities, although that antipathy was
religious as well as racial and political.

And here let me say at once, deliberately and
without hesitation, that if the racial crimes and
outrages which are of daily occurrence in the
Southern States were taking place in a semi-
civilised part of Europe, and were only half as
well advertised as the events in Bulgaria were,
the public sentiment of Europe would at once
insist upon, and would within six months secure,
reform, even at the cost of war. Such a situation
as sullies the South is a disgrace to the fair name
of Anglo-Saxon civilisation. It is not for me to
attempt to apportion the blame. Doubtless there
are grave faults on both sides. As an unprejudiced observer, I can merely declare generally that the condition of affairs is not only a

scandal so far as the United States are concerned, but also a matter of which all civilised humanity has cause to be ashamed.

It was my good fortune in the course of my tour to meet, and to confer very intimately with, the anonymous author of the most remarkable book that has yet appeared upon the Race Question. I mean "An Appeal to Pharaoh," a volume published in the winter of 1889 in New York by Messrs. Fords, Howard, and Hulbert. To this volume I must make further allusion when I come to consider the difficult, but inevitable, problem—what is to be done? At present I mention it incidentally for the reason that I am anxious to repeat here something that its writer said to me, and for the reason that all who have read the work will, I am sure, extend due deference to any opinion expressed by so competent and unbiassed an authority. My friend knows the South as few know it, and he has for the negro a genuine and kindly regard ; yet, said he, "if the option were offered me of taking my wife and family into one of the black country districts of the South, or into a jungle full of wild beasts, and if I were obliged to leave them without proper protection, I would unhesitatingly choose the jungle." I did not ask why. I knew that it was because no white woman

J 2

is safe, from hour to hour, in those black country districts. It was because the race war on the black man's side is waged largely, though not exclusively, against the whites who are least capable of self-protection, and whose safety is held most precious by those to whom they are near and dear. I am bound to produce evidence concerning this awful phase of the struggle; and, unfortunately, there is evidence in plenty ready to my hand. "Lynched for the usual crime" is a stereotyped heading in many scores of Southern newspapers. Nor, as a rule, is the brutality of the negro's act much less conspicuous than the speed and cruelty with which the victim is avenged. On both sides it is a terrible and almost unparalleled state of affairs. I will restrict myself to the recital at length of one case only :—

"Louisville, Kentucky, September 2nd, 1889.—The *Courier Journal* has a special from Somerset, Kentucky, which states that news has reached there of a brutal outrage committed upon the twelve-year-old daughter of William Oates, a prominent and wealthy farmer residing a few miles from Montecello. Mr. Oates has two daughters, aged respectively twelve and fourteen years. Mr. and Mrs. Oates left home on business, and left the two young girls in charge of the house. Mr. Oates had in his employ a negro boy about grown. Knowing that the old folks were away, he entered the house, and, after locking the door upon the two girls, assaulted the younger.

The elder girl escaped from the room, and, going to a neighbour's house, gave the alarm. A posse was organised and
started in pursuit. The negro was caught in the woods and
tied to a stake. A rail pen was then built around him, coal
oil was poured over him and upon the rails, matches were
applied, and the negro was burnt to death."

Similar outrages are, practically, of every-day
occurrence. All of them do not get into the newspapers. Many families, unwilling to publish their
disgrace and misfortune, bear their trouble in
silence. Many of the criminals, too, are never
caught: but here is proof of the commonness of
such crimes as the above. All the cases alluded
to took place during 1890, and, as will be seen,
within a very short period, and all were chronicled
in the newspapers:

On October 30th, near Valdosta, Lowndes
County, Georgia, a negro, named Lowe, assaulted
a Miss Hardee. He was arrested, but taken from
the officers the same night by a mob of whites,
tied to a tree, and shot to death.

On November 1st, eight miles from Columbia,
South Carolina, and a mile and a-half from the
Winnsboro Road, a negro attempted to assault
and then murdered Miss Florence Hornsby, aged
sixteen. A youth named Hagood was arrested
for the crime. Six years before, this youth's
father had been lynched near Woodward's store,

at Rockton, for assaulting a lady of Fairfield County.

On November 3rd, in Twigg's County, Georgia, a Miss Howell, aged seventeen, was assaulted by a negro named Owen Jones, who, having been caught and having confessed, was hung by citizens on a tree on the road from Hawkinsville to Allentown, fifty shots being then fired into his body.

On November 6th, Mrs. J. G. Bailey, of Arlington, Tennessee, was killed by a negro, who escaped, pursued by a posse of citizens intent upon lynching him.

On the night of November 8th, at Annapolis, Maryland, threats were made to lynch a coloured man named Forbes, who was in custody there for having assaulted a white girl. Revolvers were freely drawn, and a serious riot between whites and blacks was only prevented by the calling out of the Governor's Guards.

On November 17th, a negro named Henry Smith, who a few days before had assaulted one Mrs. Calhoun, was lynched near Chin's Trestle, Alabama. Another negro was lynched near Hillman, Alabama, on the same day.

Early in the morning of November 18th, a negro named William Singleton was lynched at Macon, Georgia, for an attempted assault upon the daughter of the late Chief Justice Lumpkin.

Singleton was hanged, and two volleys of pistol shots were fired into the body.

I might, if the topic were not so repulsive, cite hundreds of other examples. What I have written is, I imagine, quite sufficient to show that the situation of white women in many parts of the South is a very perilous one. Nor is this all. Throughout the South, and even elsewhere, the negro is as ready to kill the white man as the white man is to kill him. I have mentioned in the last chapter a number of cases in which, speaking generally, the whites were to blame. Here are some cases, all of recent occurrence, in most of which the initiative seems to have come, directly or indirectly, from the blacks, although the savagery displayed was often about equal on both sides :—

On October 18th, 1890, at Winston, North Carolina, a white gentleman named Silas Riggs was attacked in the street by a mob of negroes. He took refuge in a bar-room. The negroes followed and "dared" him to come out. A few whites who were in the room sallied forth, a fight ensued, Mr. Riggs was killed, and several other people were badly wounded.

On October 21st-22nd, 1890, in Ware County, Georgia, a dispute concerning land arose. Thomas Seers, one of the disputants, shot a negro. The negroes retaliated, killing B. E. M'Lendon, F. Seers, and T. Seers, and wounding another white. The despatch announcing this to the Charleston *World* says:—" Much of the territory is covered with dense pine forests, the working of which for turpentine employs large numbers of both white and black. These are very illiterate, and there is much race prejudice, which frequently leads to conflicts."

" Opelika, Alabama, October 26th, 1890.— Bob Redding, the notorious negro desperado, who has been sought for ten years, was shot and killed at three o'clock this morning by Policeman Gibson."

On October 27th, 1890, at the Jing-a-Ling Saloon, North College Street, Nashville, Tennessee, a coloured man named Lee asked the bartender for a tin of oysters, and was refused. He left, but returned with a stone, which he attempted to throw. Before he could do so the white, whose name was William Young, shot him dead.

On November 1st, 1890, at Greenville, South Carolina, a negro named Sam Swinger struck with an axe a white man named P. M. Connelly, who died a few days afterwards from his injuries.

On November 4th, 1890, near Lexington, Georgia, at a negro " hot supper," a negro, named Willis Collins, quarrelled with a white, named Wheless, who shot him with a pistol.

On November 4th, 1890, election day, at Irwine, Estill County, Kentucky, a white, named Dr. P. A. Lilly, brought up to the polls a negro, named Charles White. John Wilson, Commissioner of Schools for the county, challenged White's right to vote. Upon this Lilly and Wilson quarrelled and drew their pistols. Wilson was hit twice, but was still able to fire twice, one of his bullets striking Lilly near the heart. Then William, a brother of John Wilson, intervened, and took away Lilly's pistol. Lilly, however, drew a large knife and thrice stabbed John. A brother of Dr. Lilly also intervened, but John Wilson, lying in his blood, fired at and fatally wounded him, and, dragging himself across to where Dr. Lilly lay, dashed out Lilly's brains with his pistol. Several bystanders were slightly wounded; the two Lillys and John Wilson died.

On November 8th, 1890, at Fairmount, near Marion, Indiana, on the occasion of a Democratic *fête*, a negro named Tom Uttley interfered in the proceedings. A white named W. H. Campbell defied him, and both drew their pistols and fired simultaneously. Each had fired two harmless shots, when a white named Con Paul flung a brick at the negro, who turned and shot him dead. Another negro, named Rayser, came to the assistance of Uttley, and was shot through the left leg and right arm. Uttley fled, but was captured. In the *mêlée*, besides Paul and Rayser, four men were seriously wounded.

It cannot, I think, be necessary to say much more in order to prove the existence in the United States of race prejudice of a very dangerous and inflammable sort. The Southern white may be as well off, as regards the negro, as he deserves to be; but, nevertheless, his position and the position of his womankind are not enviable; and it tends to—nay, a large body of the negroes intend that it shall—become worse. Here is what appeared in August, 1889, in a newspaper called the *Independent*, which was published in Selma, Alabama, under the editorship of a negro preacher, named Bryan :—

" Were you (the whites) to leave this Southland, in twenty years it would be one of the grandest sections of the globe. We would show you mossback-crackers how to run a country. You would never see convicts, half-starved, depriving honest working-men of an honest living. It is only a matter of time when throughout this whole State affairs will be changed, and, I hope, to your sorrow. We were never destined to be always servants, but, like all other races, will and must have our day. You now have yours. You have had your revolutionary and civil wars, and we here predict that at no very distant day we will have our war, and we hope, as God intends, that we will be strong enough to wipe you out of existence, or hardly leave enough of you to tell the story."

And yet the armchair theorists of the North say :—" All is well; the race question in the South may now safely be left to settle itself." It will never settle itself, unless by wholesale bloodshed.

One must have lived in the South to appreciate the ever-widening gap that exists between the races. One must have lived in the South to appreciate the strength of the passions that lie half slumbering there, but are always ready to awake. Here, by way of partial illustration, is a summary of a speech which was made in September, 1889, in the Georgia Senate by Senator Gibbs, in favour of the repeal of the law prohibiting emigration agents from working in the State, his idea being to facilitate coloured emigration. Senator Gibbs claimed that the State would not be ruined by the loss of a race of people who, in their emancipated condition, were unfit for labourers. The free negro, he said, was worthless as a labourer. Emancipated, he became useless and lapsed into barbarous Voodooism. He quoted figures to sustain the position that freedom had destroyed the negroes' usefulness. Notwithstanding the great increase of blacks since the war, production had in Georgia suffered a

loss of nearly one-half. This, to him, denoted
the great demoralisation which had overtaken
negro labour, and accounted for the enormous
class of vagabond negroes whose presence in the
State was a " continual menace to property, to
peace, and to virtue." It was highly necessary,
he maintained, to get rid of this dangerous
criminal element. The lives of Southern women
were actually circumscribed and bound in, for
fear of assault at the hands of these scoundrels.
Unless something should be done to relieve the
strain which owed its existence to the presence of
these wretches, the time would come, before long,
when the white people would rise as one man
and demand emigration or extermination. " It
has only been a short time since," said he, " that
one of the villains having suffered as he deserved
at East Point, the negroes formed a plot to burn
that town and kill the citizens. Nothing was
said about that; but as soon as the whites rose to
defend themselves, and castigated some of the
plotters, the cry of ' Outrage!' was heard from
one end of the land to the other. ' Outrage on
innocent negroes,' to discourage them in their
lawlessness! I care not what course the courts
may take; when the white men strike for home
and fireside I am with them. There is not room
in this country for both the negro and the

Yankee. Vast sums have been expended to educate negroes, who have never done and will never do the State the least good. On the contrary, they are always ready, at the call of the carpet-bagger and his base Southern ally, to do her all the harm in their power."

These extracts give no notion of the viol ce of the speaker's language, but only of the tone of his speech, which admirably represented the blind intolerance of that section of Southern whites that refuses to see any good whatever in the negro, and that seems not even to recognise his humanity.

The very carelessness of the negroes on the subject of the white man's most cherished creeds and principles has more than once gone near to provoke a dreadful outbreak. The article already cited from the Selma *Independent* narrowly escaped doing so, although it contained only vulgar threats. More dangerous was an article that was printed in August, 1887, in another negro paper, the Montgomery *Herald*. " Every day or so," it said brutally, " we read of the lynching of some negro for outraging some white woman. Why is it that white women attract negro men more than in former days ? There was a time when such a thing was unheard of. There is a secret to this thing, and we greatly

suspect it is the growing appreciation of the
white Juliet for the coloured Romeo as he
becomes more and more intelligent and refined.
If something is not done to break up these lynch-
ings it will be so that after a while they will
lynch every coloured man that looks at a white
woman with a twinkle in his eye."

The writer of that article, like many of his
race, did not, one may charitably hope, realise
the attitude of the Southern white women towards
the negroes. If he did realise it, and if he knew
that no Southern white for an instant admits the
social equality of the races, he was guilty of
something very much like playing with gun-
powder. Surely the prevailing sentiment of the
whites on the subject of social equality is sufficiently indicated by the existence in many States
of laws forbidding mixed marriages, and by the
existence in all of unwritten laws which oust the
white makers of mixed unions from society, even
of the humblest and least conventional character.
The white man is blamable enough, but not the
white woman. There was much truth in a speech
of Dr. Fulton's on the subject of " The Negro's
Redemption," which I once listened to, although,
I think, he ought not to have mentioned black
women in his remarks. The chief sinners—if
sinners they can be called in such connection—

are the coloured, as distinct from the pure negro, women of the South. Dr. Fulton declared that the social relations of the whites and blacks in the South were on the same level to-day as when slavery existed; even men high in religious circles ran no risk of ostracisation when it became known they were the fathers of children by coloured concubines.

And while the armchair theorist of the North is easy in his mind with regard to the race question, concerning which he knows practically nothing, the Southern white man, who ought to know all the dangers of the situation, is, I am obliged to admit, strangely indifferent to them. His idea seems to be, " There are dangers in the future ; but the present situation will probably last as long as I live, and so I have no need to greatly worry myself about it. I do not fear the negro ; I do not believe in his power of organisation ; and if he were to rise we could crush him into resignation." He seems to be unmindful of the fact that the existence of the Black Belt in the South paralyses his material progress and fetters his whole action as a citizen. Capital does not go Southward in search of an invest-ment, or, if it go, it goes seldom, and it goes with hesitation. It has no confidence in a country which may any day fall again under the rule of a black majority, and may then drift back into the anarchy of the Reconstruction period. And, although the white man does not personally fear the negro, he so much fears him corporately that all his political principles and leanings have vanished in face of the one great question, Shall the white rule or the black ?

The Southern whites form to-day one political party. Their point of union is not the tariff, not civil service reform, not the pension system, but simply and solely the one question. The penalty is that now for years past one party has been continuously in power throughout the Solid South, and that it has had practically no opposition. This is an unwholesome state of public affairs ; it would be undesirable anywhere. In America it is particularly dangerous, for it tends to corrupt. The Southern State Governments are, it must be admitted, better and purer than, in the circumstances, might be reasonably expected ; but every intelligent Southerner sees and feels the bad influence.

The South, however, has a choice of two evils, and she has chosen the least. She is not responsible for the situation. She can only make the best of it. An illustration of what I mean was afforded during the 1890 elections in South Carolina. The two candidates for Governor were

Haskell and Tillman. Haskell is an honoured veteran of the war, a tried statesman, a general favourite, and an upright and courteous gentleman. Tillman's experience of arms is confined to participation in a race riot; he is new to politics; he is the favourite only of the lower and least reputable class of whites; and his election utterances betray him as glaringly deficient in tact and gravely lacking in conventional politeness. Both are Democrats. It was Tillman's fortune, thanks to the influence of the Farmers' Alliance, to be the nominee of the Democratic Convention; and on that point the whole contest turned. All the best men in the State wanted Haskell, and did not want Tillman; but Haskell had been offered Republican support, and so, rather than vote for Haskell, the best men either abstained or voted for Tillman. It would never do, they felt, to allow Haskell to come into power on a wave which was partially composed of negro and Republican votes. Party discipline, therefore, prevailed over personal preference, and the worse man won. But for the presence of a negro majority in South Carolina, Haskell would no doubt have been elected. How true it is, as Jefferson said, that American institutions are founded on jealousy and distrust, and not on confidence!

K

Yet, although the white resents the presence of the black, and forbids the black to fully exercise such rights as the Federal Government has conferred upon him, the white is, withal, more dependent to-day upon the negro than the negro is upon the white. There can be no question that the sudden removal to-morrow of every white man from the Black Belt would cause far less inconvenience to the negroes than the sudden removal of every black and coloured man would cause to the whites. The needs of the negro are small, and he can supply most of them by his own exertion. The needs of the white man are relatively large, and he has been for generations accustomed to have most of them supplied to him by the exertion of the negro—first as slave, and, for the last quarter of a century, as very lightly paid freedman. The result is that in certain spheres of labour the negro is supreme throughout the South. He has no white rivals, for the reason that the wages which content him would be scorned by the lowest and poorest white in the country. His disappearance, therefore, would leave those particular spheres—the cottonfield, the plantations, the domestic servants' department, and many more—absolutely empty. In a word, without the negro, or without, at least, some substitute for the negro, the

Southern white would for a time be in danger of starving.

Let me not be here understood to mean that upon the whole the South is unsuitable as the white man's home. It is, on the contrary, a fit home and, in most parts, a healthy one for him. The death-rate per thousand inhabitants in the eight most distinctively Southern States is given in the 1880 census report as follows : Alabama, 14·20; Arkansas, 18·46; Florida, 11·72; Georgia, 13·97; Louisiana, 15·44; Mississippi, 12·89; North Carolina, 15·39; and South Carolina, 15·80. These are the swampy, malarial States, commonly accounted most pestilential in climate. Compare their death-rates with those of eight other States commonly accounted salubrious in climate: Indiana, 15·78; Kansas, 15·22; Massachusetts, 18·59; New Hampshire, 16·09; New Jersey, 16·33; New York, 17·38; Rhode Island, 17; and Illinois, 14·63. The comparison is not unfavourable to the South; and it must be borne in mind that the death-rates given for the Southern States named include negroes as well as whites, a fact which enormously swells the average, for the reason that the negro death-rate is much higher than the white, and in many cases more than doubles it.

The fact that the menial work of the South is done by the negro, combined with the fact

K 2

that the black race is despised by the white, is
responsible for the existence in the South of a
class of whites such as is met with nowhere else
in the United States ; I mean the poor and idle
and unashamed class. These people will not
undertake menial work as we understand it.
They believe that, if they did so, they would
ipso facto place themselves on a level with the
negroes.

The upshot is that the Southern white man is,
as a rule, either a " boss," (that is, an employer of
labour) or a "loafer." The " boss " is generally
a good citizen ; the " loafer " is uniformly a bad
one, but he seems to be a necessary product of
the situation. The presence of the negro has
created him, and he is a very dangerous factor
in the race problem. He is the man who preys
upon the community, white as well as black. He
deems it more worthy of his white manhood to
be a gambler, a corrupt political adventurer, a
haunter of low saloons, a braggart and a swag-
gerer, than to work for a poor but honest living.
And even the white man who is not a " loafer,"
but a "boss," is often enough a very small "boss"
indeed—the farmer of a few thin and infertile
acres—a citizen who is only a "boss" because, for
race reasons, he is too proud to accept employment. In one of the North-Western States he

would naturally be a " farm-hand," and would be much better off than he is, as his own master, in Georgia or Mississippi.

The result of this condition of affairs is that in the Black Belt wealth is less equally divided than it is elsewhere. There is the small class of white capitalists, there is the larger class of poor whites, and there is the still larger class of negroes, most of whom live literally from hand to mouth. The war is, of course, partially responsible for a certain amount of white poverty; but the main cause is, as I have said, the presence of the negro; and upon poverty and false pride follows ignorance. There is more white ignorance in the South than in any other part of the States. The average percentage of white illiteracy among people of ten years old and upwards in the Northern States in 1880 was 5·2; and it varied from 3·5 in Nebraska, 3·6 in Oregon, 3·7 in Kansas, and 3·8 in Iowa, to 7·0 in Indiana and 10·9—a wholly exceptional figure—in Rhode Island. But the average percentage of white illiteracy among people of ten years old and up-wards in the States of the Black Belt in 1880 was 22·2, the percentage in the individual States being—Mississippi, 16·3; Virginia, 18·2; Louisiana, 18·4; Florida, 19·9; South Carolina, 21·9; Georgia, 22·9; Alabama, 24·7; and North

Carolina, 31·5. And this comparison, significant as it is, does not show the whole extent of Southern white illiteracy, for the figures above given refer not merely to the native, but also to the foreign-born population. Putting aside the latter, one finds that while the average native white illiteracy in the North was but 3·2 per cent., that in the South was 24·7 per cent. Thus, of every four native-born whites in the Black Belt, three only even pretended to be able to read and write. The proportion of native white illiterates in the whole North was no more than one in thirty-one. In Massachusetts it was considerably less than one in a hundred. So much for the demoralising influence of the situation upon the white man. I have now to review some of the suggested solutions to the race problem.

CHAPTER V.

WHEN freedom was first given to the Slaves in the South, no one suspected that the measure was destined to create a new and more difficult phase of a problem which had already brought the Union to the verge of ruin. Nearly every one believed that manumission would, in course of time, solve the race question; and those who did not believe that manumission alone would produce this result, were apparently convinced that manumission combined with extension of the suffrage, and with the concession of full rights of citizenship to the freedmen, could not possibly fail to be efficacious; and so Amendment XV. was passed as a final panacea.

But, in fairness to the foresight of a discerning minority, it should be remembered that the amendment was not passed unanimously. It was rejected by California, Delaware, Kentucky, Indiana, Oregon, and Tennessee, and later, on reflection, by New York. It is true that it was

ultimately ratified by 29 out of 37 States.
Several of these were, however, at the time under
" Reconstruction," and the ratification from Virginia, South Carolina, North Carolina, Georgia,
Florida, Alabama, Mississippi, Louisiana, Arkansas, and Texas, may be supposed to have been
to some extent exacted under duress.   Still, the
question of giving suffrage to the negro was not
then anywhere regarded from the point of view
from which it is now seen by the best men of all
parties.   As Judge Tourgée has pointed out, it
was confidently predicted by every theorist who
speculated upon the subject, that the negro would
wither away under the influences of freedom and
civilisation.   It was unhesitatingly asserted, and
almost universally believed, that the first decade
of liberty would show the race to have been deci-
mated by disease, debauchery, and the lack of the
master's paternal care.   It was not an unnatural
conclusion for men to arrive at who devoutly
believed in the negro's incapacity for self-support.
Mr. Tourgée adds :—

" That the people of the North should believe it also is
hardly to be wondered at.   They have always reflected the
Southern idea of the negro in everything, except as to his natural
right to be free and to exercise the rights of the freeman.
The North, however, has never desired the numerical
preponderance of the coloured man, and has especially desired

to avoid responsibility in regard thereto. From the first it seems to have been animated by a sneaking notion that after having used the negro to fight its battles, freed him as the natural result of the overthrow of a rebellion based on slavery, and enfranchised him to constitute a political foil to the ambition and disloyalty of his former master, it could at any time unload him upon the States where he chanced to dwell, wash its hands of all further responsibility in the matter, and leave him to live or die as chance might determine. It seems a hard saying, but there is very little doubt that, side by side with the belief in the Northern mind that the negro would disappear beneath the glare of civilisation, was a half-conscious feeling that such disappearance would be a very simple and easy solution of a troublesome question.

It being, then, the prevalent and all but general impression that the negro would soon die out, it scarcely occurred to legislators to question whether or nor it might complicate matters to make him, for his short season on earth, a full voting citizen. Had it been foreseen that, far from dying out, the negro would increase and multiply to an almost unheard-of extent, there would, we may be sure, have been much more hesitation than there was over the passing of Amendment XV. That amendment may be repealed at any time by the action of two-thirds of both Houses of Congress, and by subsequent ratification by three-fourths of the States of the Union; but to look for its repeal now is hopeless.

Colonel T. B. Edgington, a Northerner, recognising the menace of negro suffrage to Southern civilisation, proposed, in a speech delivered at Memphis in June, 1889, to get over this phase of the difficulty by limiting the right to vote among the negroes, and by making the office of voter, or suffragist among them, an elective office—an office that a man shall hold, say for four years, by election of the whole body of the people, or by election of the coloured people alone, if this course seem preferable. Thus no property or educational qualification would be required. The end desired could be attained by so adjusting and limiting the negro vote that it should not exceed say 5 or 10 per cent. of the white vote on any given question or issue.

There have been many other advocates in favour of limitation or suspension of negro suffrage; and a movement towards this end has lately made much progress in Mississippi; but, upon the whole, it seems to me that, as I have said, to look for the repeal of Amendment XV. is hopeless.

Nor would its repeal at the present date solve the difficulty. It would rather accentuate it; for the negro would not submit to be thus set back upon his upward path. Indeed, repeal of the Amendment is even more ridiculous as a remedy than is another measure which, nevertheless, has more than once been advocated by speakers and writers who ought to have known better—I mean the extermination of the inconvenient race : for, whereas extermination would be undoubtedly effective, repeal would only reopen the difficulty in a new and inflamed phase.

Neither policy is to be seriously considered. The United States have, both as individual States and as a Union, incurred towards the negro liabilities which cannot be repudiated or shirked. The country kidnapped and imported the negro, enslaved him or connived at his enslavement, used him for national purposes, freed him and put power into his hands ; and it cannot now or ever shake off all responsibility concerning him. As he is, he is, for many reasons, an undesirable fellow-citizen ; but he was created a fellow-citizen to suit the temporary political interests of the North ; and, having served those interests, he is not now to be disowned and cast out a beggar. Equality between the races is a hopeless dream ; yet the whole fabric of American institutions rests upon the assumed equality of the citizens. If American institutions honestly and freely tolerated the existence of "classes," the race question would never have attained its present importance. The negro, while "keeping his place," might still have enjoyed his vote. As things stand, he is practically, in spite of his nominal rights, an alien. When, as in the Reconstruction Period, he exercised his rights most fully, he did so to the prejudice of the rights of the Southern white, who was then, as it were, the alien. Now, when the white Southerner has fully resumed the exercise of his rights, the black man suffers proportionately. And every day's experience shows more and more clearly that real equality in the South, as between whites and blacks, is impossible of attainment. Says the New York *Tribune*, with bitterness but with truth :—

"There may be one faith, one baptism, and one name under Heaven whereby men may be saved, but in South Carolina there must be a white man's church, high-toned and very respectable, and a place somewhere outside where the negroes may herd together without disturbing the pious meditations of their superiors. Simon of Cyrene, who carried the cross, was a negro, but that passage in the Gospels can be bracketed if need be, and not read in the white churches of Charleston during Holy Week. The Ethiopian eunuch baptised by Philip could not have had a white skin, but that chapter can be omitted in the liturgical order of second lessons. The white saints will kindly consent to pray every Sunday for all sorts and conditions of men, provided 'the niggers' are taught to remain in their own place and not to intrude where they are not wanted. They will live and die in the faith and communion of their white fathers and white grandfathers, with no negroes on the sacred premises, except possibly the coloured sexton, who must not under any circumstances be a communicant, but merely a sweep. What arrangements will be made for their benefit in the next world they cannot tell, but they may at least indulge the pious hope that there will be a separate 'nigger heaven'—an adjunct, like their own coloured convention, to the white man's paradise—a separate missionary jurisdiction with swarthy angels and combination negro melodies."

I would merely add, by way of comment, that Charleston and South Carolina are by no means the most intolerant and intolerable places in which the Southern negro is at present dwelling.

I have alluded to two suggested, but ineffective or impracticable, ways out of the difficulty. Another scheme, from which in the early days of the negro's freedom much was expected, was the gradual fusion of the races. Miscegenation, or intermarriage between whites and blacks, was, for a season, the favourite prescription of theorists, especially in the North, whence to this moment comes plenty of theory, with little or no practical help. Another suggested remedy was education. If, said the counsellors, you educate the negro thoroughly well, you will render him as good a citizen as the white man. Let me deal separately with each of these plans, as well as with yet another—namely, the surrender of the Black Belt to the black, and the constitution of

recognised Black States as members of the
Union. I will deal with them in the order in
which they appear to have found favour, and first
with the least promising.

Surrender, no matter in what form it may be
advocated and brought about, involves the un-
justifiable premiss that the negro is fit for self-
government. It has never been proposed that the
States of the Black Belt, or any portion of them,
shall be allowed independence. No one has gone
further than to suggest that the whites, or the
great body of whites, shall retire from them with
indemnity. The relationship of the States to the
Union would remain as at present. The State
government and representation would simply be
left to the negroes and the coloured people, the
rights of such whites as might elect to stay being,
of course, as much as possible secured. The
lessons of history and experience are, in the
highest degree, discouraging for the success of
such a scheme, could it, which I very much
doubt, be carried out in its initial stages. Says
Mr. J. A. Froude, in " The English in the West
Indies ":—

"There is a saying in Hayti that the white man has no
rights which the blacks are bound to recognise. . . . They
can own no freehold property, and exist only on tolerance.
They are called ' white trash.' Black dukes and marquises

drive over them in the street and swear at them. . . . .
Englishmen move about Jacmel as if they were ashamed of
themselves among their dusky lords and masters. The presence
of Europeans in any form is barely tolerated."

And here is the same writer's summary of the
history of San Domingo:—

"St. Domingo, of which Hayti is the largest division, was
the earliest island discovered by Columbus, and the finest in
the Caribbean Ocean. The Spaniards found there a million or
two of mild and innocent Indians, whom . . . they con-
verted off the face of the earth, working them to death in their
mines and plantations. They filled their places with blacks
from Africa. They colonised, they built cities ; they throve
and prospered for nearly two hundred years, when Hayti was
taken from them and made a French province. The French
kept it till the Revolution. They built towns, they laid out
farms and sugar fields, they planted coffee all over the island,
where it now grows wild. Vast herds of cattle roamed over
the mountains, splendid houses rose over the rich savannahs.
The French Church put out its strength ; there were churches
and priests in every parish. So firm was the hold that they
had gained that Hayti, like Cuba, seemed to have been made a
part of the old world, and as civilised as France itself. The
Revolution came, and the reign of Liberty. The blacks took
arms ; they surprised the plantations ; they made a clean sweep
of the whole French population. . . . The island being
thus derelict, Spain and England both tried their hands to
recover it, but failed ; . . . and a black nation, with a
Republican Constitution, and a population, perhaps, of about a
million and a half of pure-blood negroes, has since been in un-
challenged possession, and has arrived at the condition which
has been described to us by Sir Spenser St. John."

What that condition is has been painted in
lurid, but not exaggerated, colours by Sir
Spenser, to whose book reference should be
made. Mr. Froude sufficiently sketches it in the
following passages :—

" Morals in the technical sense they have none."

" A religion which will keep the West Indian blacks from
falling back into devil-worship is still to seek."

" In spite of schools and missionaries, 70 per cent. of the
children now born among them are illegitimate."

" Behind the religiosity, there lies active and alive the
horrible revival of the Western African superstitions; the
serpent-worship, and the child sacrifice, and the cannibalism.
The facts are notorious."

" There is no sign, not the slightest, that the generality of
the race are improving either in intelligence or moral habits ;
all the evidence is the other way."

" Ninety years of negro self-government have had their use
in showing what it really means. . . . The movement is
backward, not forward."

Not only in St. Domingo has the experiment
of negro self-government been tried under
pseudo-civilised conditions. It has been tried
also in Liberia, and with almost equally bad
results. To-day in Liberia whites are treated
by the blacks much as blacks are treated by
whites in the South. A negro State has never
yet shown itself worthy to rank on terms of
equality with a white one, and there are no

symptoms that it will ever reach that level. Diplomatic intercourse with such States cannot be carried on under ordinary conditions; neither can commercial transactions. Black rule means anarchy, and it invariably brings to the front the fact that the negro hates the white as much as the white hates him, and is even more ready than the white is to play the tyrant and the oppressor. Life for a white in every existing negro State is well-nigh unendurable. A fringe of negro States on the southern and south-eastern borders of the Union would, therefore, be a perpetual danger to the whole Federation.

Education is a supposed panacea that has been more widely advocated; and amongst its ablest champions is Judge Tourgée. But education, although it may in time civilise and soften the more naturally intelligent of the coloured people, will, I am convinced, do very little for the pure-blooded negro, the man with the facial angle of about 70 deg. You cannot make a silk purse out of a sow's ear, and you cannot make a Solon out of a person with an unsuitably constructed head. Coloured people and blacks in the South have now for quite twenty years been more or less subjected to the influences of education. Almost anyone who may have so desired has been able during that period, and, indeed, for a longer time, to

L

obtain instruction of all kinds—technical, lin-
guistic, mathematical, scientific, and philosophical, as well as elementary. In fact, there is in
the South even less practical difficulty in the way
of the poor negro of genius, if such a being exist,
than in the way of the poor white of genius; for
philanthropic people have established free colleges
and schools for him, and stand ready to give him
all possible encouragement to persevere and make
a name and a fortune. Yet, in spite of this, the
pure-blooded negroes who have come to the front
in any way may be counted on one's fingers—
perhaps on the fingers of one hand. A greater
number of coloured people—mulattoes and cross-
breeds of various tinctures—have profited by the
opportunities given. Among these, one of the
most noteworthy is Mr. B. K. Bruce, of Mississippi. He was born of slave parents in Virginia,
in 1841, and went to Mississippi in his boyhood,
subsequently removing to Missouri, but returning
in 1869. His education was limited, and while
following the occupation of a planter, he held the
position of Sergeant-at-Arms of the State Senate
for two years, Sheriff and Tax Collector of
Bolivar County for four years, a Levée Commissioner for three years, and was elected to the
U.S. Senate in 1875. He now holds a responsible Government post at Washington. Another

notable coloured man is Mr. F. Douglass, who is
many times mentioned in these pages, and who
is now United States Minister to Hayti. He
had previously been one of the San Domingo
Commissioners; was a trustee of the Howard
University and of the Freedman's Bank, and was
appointed United States Marshal for the District
of Columbia by President Hayes, and Recorder
of Deeds for the District by President Garfield.
He is the fourth coloured Minister to Hayti, his
predecessors having been Messrs. E. D. Bassett,
J. U. Langston, and J. E. W. Thompson. Mr.
R. B. Elliott, a coloured man who was born at
Boston and educated in England, has held several
high positions in South Carolina, including a seat
in the Forty-second and Forty-third Congress,
from which he resigned. Mr. Pinchback, Lieu-
tenant Governor of Louisiana, who afterwards
contested a seat in the Senate, is another of the
leading coloured men.

But these are not the individuals with the
negro facial angle and the full negro characteristics, neither do they form the majority
of the negro and negroid population. Moreover, they are, I am assured, decreasing in
numbers, and, although more intelligent than the
pure blacks, are, as a general rule, even less
desirable as citizens. But of this later. Suffice

L 2

it to say that education has not produced such
results as might fairly be expected from it; and
that the educated man of colour, if severed from
white influence and stimulus, seems to evince an
ineradicable tendency to "hark back" to the
vices, the superstitions, and the weaknesses of his
ancestors; while, as I have already said, education
does not abolish race-prejudice, and scarcely
ameliorates it. The educated black becomes
doubly conscious of the contempt in which the
whites hold him and his race; while the white
looks upon the educated black as a doubly
dangerous rival and possible enemy. In the
meantime, with every scrap of education that he
assimilates, the black imbibes increased anxiety
to assume that position as a citizen which the
white is, above all things, determined that the
coloured man shall never hold in the South.
Even the Boston *Transcript*, a Northern paper,
recognises this fact. "We have always said," it
declares, "that the very improvement of the
negroes' condition socially makes worse the prospect of quieting down that burning question.
Naturally, the more they get the more they want,
and the more they will have, too. The only
logical position was to keep them slaves. Once
citizens, they have as good right as anybody to
ride in your Pullman, or sit in your theatre or

restaurant, sleep in your hotel or church, or live in your street or block. Lack of money is all that intervenes at present, and that will not always."

And Dr. S. M. Smith, D.D., of Columbia, South Carolina, writing in the *Presbyterian Quarterly* for October, 1889, takes the same view. His conclusions are thus summed up by the Raleigh *State Chronicle* :—

"The patent panacea for all negro defects, education, does not mend matters in the least; an 'educated' negro is just as much negro as before, just the same raw hide volume with the incongruous addition of a gilt edge; he is only a little more aggressively offensive than his less ornate brother. Social complications are not at all lessened by education, nor mitigated by 'light complexions' either."

Miscegenation is the most widely favoured and venerable of what I may call the quack nostrums for the cure of existing evils. The late Mr. Henry Woodfin Grady, one of the truest friends that the negro ever had, laid it down as an axiomatic condition of harmony between races "that each race should earnestly desire a fusion of blood, in which all differences would be lost." The action of the natural law thus stated has made white North America what it is to-day. But, as the author of "An Appeal to Pharaoh" points out, the law that governs the distribution, association, and conduct of all other living creatures rules the action of men also. Birds and beasts, fishes, reptiles, and insects— nay, trees, and flowers, and weeds—group them- selves together after their kind: and man is no exception to the universal rule. In every land and clime, under whatever circumstances and con- ditions he may be placed, he recognises and obeys nature by seeking his own kind, avoiding every other, and warring with his dissimilar neighbour. Families, classes, societies, tribes, nations form around some common centre of agreement or likeness that unites the like and excludes the unlike from the invisible but impass- able circle. The map of the world is a map of the larger groups. The history of the world is chiefly the history of the formation, organisation, and contentions of these groups. The history of North America is a particular demonstration of the action of the law under consideration. Four cen- turies have not elapsed since the white man first set his foot on the eastern shore of the New World. Every step of his progress westward has been marked by the blood of the dissimilar race, which he found there and drove before him. He sits on the grave of the red man; he has shut the door in the face of the yellow man from China; what shall he do with the black man from Africa?

Intermarry with him, say the quacks. But, to again quote Mr. Grady, "not only do the two races not earnestly desire fusion, but both races are pledged against it as the one impossible thing." This is quite notorious throughout the South, where it has even inspired legislation against miscegenation; yet many humanitarian theorists in the North still put forward inter-marriage as the panacea.

I summarise here an interesting article which was contributed to *Belford's Magazine* for September, 1889, by Mr. Cone on the significance of racial colour. The writer attempts to prove that colour of the skin is inseparably connected with the brain and higher faculties of the individual, and that according to a fundamental law of Nature the negro, being black, always has been, and for ever must remain, an inferior grade of humanity. The alleged law, as stated by Mr. Cone, is as follows:—" Whatever race or species is changeless from generation to generation as to the colour of its skin, hair, and eyes—if it be man or animal—or eyes and plumage, if it be bird, evinces low brain-power, is 'inferior'; while that which is changeful from generation to generation as to the colour of its skin, hair and eyes, or plumage, shows high brain-power, is 'superior.' Or, more briefly: The invariable as to racial colour is the 'inferior'; the variable is the 'superior' race." After an elaborate investigation of attempts to domesticate wild birds and wild animals, and of efforts to raise black men and red men to a higher plane of civilisation, the conclusion is reached that all such attempts have been absolute failures. The cases of Hayti and Jamaica are cited to prove that the black man, when raised by a higher race to a level of life which he was unable to himself attain, has never shown any ability to maintain himself there; he "lacks the brain-fibre, the brain-power, which is necessary to do so, and, left to himself, he retrogrades, reverts." The red Egyptian and the yellow Chinaman, though more variable, and, therefore, of a higher type than the negro, are forcible illustrations of arrested development. "Hybridism in animals, and the sterility of miscegenation when pressed beyond certain well-known limitations, are proof that Nature punishes in her own effective way the violation of her laws, whether men have understood those laws or not." This fundamental law of Mr. Cone declares that racial intellect, racial superiority and inferiority, are written in racial colour; and the writer concludes by saying:—"If this be true, then other conclusions inevitably follow, which a wise statesmanship, sincere in purpose, lofty in motive, scholarly in grasp, and philosophic in breadth of view, will not disregard."

It is true that America has become a mighty nation from the intermingling of races, but almost entirely from the intermingling of races that belong to the Indo-Germanic stock. The more nearly allied the races, the more successful has been the intermingling. English, Scotch, Irish, Dutch, Germans, and Scandinavians have harmoniously united to produce the American; but the Latins, as we see in Canada and Louisiana, blend much less readily with the Anglo-Saxons and Celts, and continue to hold aloof long after races more nearly akin have inextricably merged in one composite but individual people. The French, the Italians, and the Spaniards are those that thus hold aloof. Some of them seem to intermarry—and this is peculiarly noticeable in Central and South America—more readily with the native Indian, or even with the negro, than with the Anglo-Saxon. In Paraguay, Guatemala, Nicaragua, Costa Rica, Salvador, Honduras, and Southern Mexico, for example, the mass of the population is Indo-Spanish. It would seem as if the Southern European does not possess the colour-antipathy as the pure white possesses it; and, surely, his own dark colour lends plausibility to the theory that he is one step nearer than the

pure white is to the Indian and negro stocks.
But nowhere does the pure white, as represented
by the Anglo-Teutonic races, generally admit
coloured races to social and family equality.
There are mulattoes in the United States, but
nearly every mulatto is the offspring not of
marriage but of an irregular, temporary, and disgraceful union. There are Eurasians in India,
where, after all, whites and coloured people are
racially related; yet even there most of the half-
breeds are illegitimate. In Africa, in the meanwhile, the Hottentot and the Bushman, instead of
blending with the whites, are vanishing. In
Australia, too, and New Zealand, the aboriginal
inhabitant is disappearing fast. Race, more than
anything else, has to this day kept Central Africa
a secret from the white world. And the
numerical superiority of the negroes in the Black
Belt is, more than anything else, responsible for
the fact that the Black Belt is almost a *terra
incognita* to the mass of Northerners, and for the
equally important fact that European and Northern brains and capital do not go there as they go
to the whiter but not richer West. In the South,
in the past five-and-twenty years, the negro has
improved in very many respects; but that makes
no radical difference. He is still the negro, and
he always will be the negro.

Yet, in spite of these and other considerations that must be ever present to the minds of all who know the South and are unprejudiced observers of what is there for them to see, we find people persistently advocating miscegenation as the certain cure for the evils of the situation. Mr. Frederick Douglass, a mulatto, and, perhaps, the most distinguished coloured American now living, takes a somewhat neutral position. Writing in the *North American Review* for May, 1886, on miscegenation, he says :—" I am not a propagandist, but a prophet. While I would not be understood as advocating the desirability of such a result, I would not be understood as deprecating it." But many whites have been bolder. The opinion of the Rev. Dr. B. T. Tanner is that " whether the whites and the blacks of the country shall mix is no longer an open question, being settled by the fact that the mixing has already, and to a large extent, taken place. . . . As we gaze," he continues, " upon the millions of whites and millions of blacks confronting each other, and as we remember that where there is no association there can be no certain amity, and that where there is no amity there can be no lasting peace, we are made to ask, What will the harvest be ? As there cannot be other than one Government, so there must not be ultimately

more than one people. The union of which we
so justly boast must comprehend both." The
Rev. J. W. Hamilton, of Boston, is another prophet and advocate of miscegenation. And the
language of Prof. S. B. Darnell, of the Cookman
Institute, Jacksonville, is:—" However we may
feel on the subject, the stern logic of sequences
will make, in the coming years, ' our brother in
black' a misnomer; and the diverse streams of
blood will so mingle that our posterity shall quote
again, 'God hath made of one blood all nations of
men.'"   On the other hand, Abraham Lincoln, in
his reply to Senator Douglas in 1857, said, " There
is a natural disgust in the minds of nearly all white
people at the idea of an indiscriminate amalgamation of the white and black races." And again:—
" There is a physical difference between the two,
which, in my judgment, will probably for ever
forbid their living together upon the footing of
perfect equality; and, inasmuch as it becomes a
necessity that there must be a difference, I, as
well as Judge Douglas, am in favour of the race
to which I belong having the superior position."
And these prejudices belong not only to the pure
white branches of the great Indo-Germanic stock.
In our West Indian colonies there are about
10,000 coolies, of whom Mr. Froude says:—" They
are proud, and will not intermarry with the

Africans. If there is no jealousy, there is no friendship. The two races are more absolutely apart than the white and the black." Between the races in America, as Judge Tourgée expresses it, "there is no equalisation, no fraternity, no assimilation of rights, no reciprocity of affection. Children may caress each other, because they are children. Betwixt adults fewer demonstrations of affection are allowed than the master bestows upon his dog. Ordinary politeness becomes a mark of shame. A caress implies degradation. In all that region no man would stand in a lady's presence unless uncovered. Yet not a white man in its borders dares lift his hat to a coloured woman in the street, no matter how pure her life, how noble her attributes, or how deep his obligations to her might be."

If such be the prevailing sentiments among Southern white people, the questioner may say, How then do you account for the mulattoes, thousands of whom are found in and far beyond the limits of the Black Belt? The point is one concerning which I am anxious to convey a very clear understanding, for it is a most important point. There is, undoubtedly, a large mixed population; and, as the Rev. Dr. T. B. Tanner has said, "the mixing has already taken place." It has taken place; it took place amid conditions

which have ceased to exist; and practically it
takes place no longer. It is in his assumption
that the mixing process continues, and in his im-
plied assumption that the causative unions were
at any period and to any considerable extent
legitimate ones, that Dr. Tanner creates a false
impression. Here are the facts, so far as I have
been able to ascertain them ; and I have spared
no pains in my efforts to get at the bottom of
them.

The mulatto, strictly classified, is the offspring
of a pure white and a pure black parent, and he
is much less common than is generally supposed.
In nine hundred and ninety-nine cases out of a
thousand he is of illegitimate birth, and in ninety-
nine cases out of a hundred, except, perhaps, in
Louisiana, where there is a large population of
French descent and of modified anti-negro prejudices, he is a person no longer a minor. I
made inquiries in Charleston with the object of
discovering there a mulatto child of tender years,
but in vain. I found mulattoes of five-and-twenty
or thirty, but I could find no children. More
than once in the street I thought that I had come
upon what I was looking for ; but in every case
the child proved to be not a genuine mulatto, but
simply a coloured child, the offspring, that is, of
a parent or parents with some white blood, but

not the direct offspring of black and white. The coloured people, as distinct from the pure-blooded negroes, are everywhere common enough, and may be casually mistaken by the unfamiliar observer for mulattoes. But the real mulatto is comparatively rare, and is daily becoming rarer. Most of the coloured people have less than one-half white blood; an overwhelming majority, indeed, have less than one-quarter. A coloured person with but one-eighth or one-sixteenth of negro blood is very rare indeed. The kind of proportion that is common is ten-twelfths or fourteen-sixteenths, or even more. All this points to the fact that miscegenation, although at one time prevalent, has, as I have said, practically ceased. It also points to the fact that, as the author of "An Appeal to Pharaoh" puts it :—

"The process is never continued beyond a few steps further, and halts abruptly at the point where it promises to prove effective by the obliteration of the negro type in an individual who shall still represent the union of the two diverse strains of blood. Such an individual may, indeed, exist in America; but, if so, he wisely holds his peace as to his pedigree. The octoroon is nearly white, and is usually attractive in person. He is free to marry in his own class, or below it ; but he is as far from marrying a white woman as was his blackest ancestor. And so of the mythical individual, whose case we have just considered."

The truth is that the mulatto, the quadroon, and the octoroon are chiefly products of the slavery period. Since the war, the birth of a mulatto, quadroon, or octoroon out of wedlock has been of the rarest occurrence; and legislation and prejudice have limited, and well-nigh put a stop to, the birth of these people in wedlock. Mulattoes intermarry, and, in some cases, have intermarried for generations. In more than one place in the South they, with occasional admixture of quadroons, constitute a small, distinct community of highly respectable people, living to themselves for the most part, and having as little in common with their black as with their white neighbours; for white blood, even in small quantities, " tells," and the pride of the mulatto or quadroon, as a rule, rebels as much at the idea of alliance with the negro as does the pride of the white at the idea of alliance with coloured or black. The mulatto originated in the desire of the slave woman to enjoy the favour of her white master, and in the desire of the master to add to his possessions—as well as, to some extent, in white brutality and youthful dissoluteness, at a period when these could be very freely indulged. The black slave woman and the white master have disappeared, and all the conditions have changed. With the changed conditions the birth of mulattoes, of quadroons, and of octoroons has steadily grown rarer and rarer, until it threatens to cease altogether. If miscegenation ever promised to solve the negro problem—and this I doubt — emancipation hopelessly destroyed the prospect. Whatever miscegenation there was, was entirely confined to white men and negro or coloured women. The Southern white woman has had no part in it. In her opinion it is, in all circumstances and conditions, loathsome and abominable. Miscegenation, upon the only principles in accordance with which it has ever been practised between the races in the United States, is, after all, no real miscegenation at all. It was one-sided, it was criminal, it involved the disowning of the child by the stronger of its parents. Could any satisfactory admixture have been effected on such terms? And there has never been the slightest sign of assimilation on any other terms.

There is yet another aspect of the question, and that is, Is the mulatto, the quadroon, the octoroon, a desirable product? It cannot be denied that the intelligence, the general aptitude for affairs, the business and political capacity, the æsthetic faculty, and the finer qualities of the coloured man, are always closely proportionate to the degree of whiteness of his skin. In the

M

coloured man we continually find a perception
of artistic beauty in form, colour, and effect, and
what may be called a natural sense of decency
and shame.   These are foreign to the negro
nature; and their peculiar absence seems to widen
the already sufficiently broad gulf between pure
black and pure white.   In the coloured man,
again, we find the natural leader of the negro in
all movements, political, religious, and social.
The only representative of the coloured population who ever sat in the United States Senate was
nearly white; and in the Reconstruction period
the masters of the situation in the South were,
not Northern whites and Southern negroes, but
Northern whites and Southern coloured men.
The hybrid of the white man's begetting was
then the white man's scourge.   Beyond a doubt,
he is intellectually a great improvement upon the
black.   But he is no nearer the white than was
his black mother.   "If," says the author of " An
Appeal to Pharaoh," "the negro race were wholly
supplanted on American soil by a race of mulattoes, or even of octoroons, the race problem would
be so far from approaching a solution, that it
would be at least as perplexing and as fraught
with present difficulty and promise of future
trouble as is the negro problem of to-day."   And,
apart from this, the mulatto is physically and

constitutionally, and also to, I fear, a very large extent, morally, a failure. Although both white and negro are long-lived races, the mulatto, born of Anglo-Saxon and negro, very rarely attains the age of fifty; and he is particularly and abnormally subject to certain forms of disease. Moreover, there is a general and, I believe, a not unfounded impression that nature refuses to perpetuate beyond two or three generations this race of human hybrids. Dr. J. C. Knott, after nearly fifty years of residence among the black and white races of the South, declared mulattoes to be " the shortest-lived of any class of the human family," and that the product of the cross between the Anglo-Saxon and the negro dies off before the dark stain can be washed out by amalgamation; while Professor Drummond says, " Inappropriate hybridism is checked by the law of sterility." This last doctrine may, it is just possible, not apply, or may only apply to a limited extent, to the mulatto. There is, unfortunately, less room for doubt that, in the South, people of mixed blood furnish a surprisingly and disproportionately large quota to the criminal population. It was estimated that in the Mississippi Penitentiary, on the 1st of December, 1885, there was one white for every 4,480 white inhabitants of the State, one black for every 918 black

M 2

inhabitants, and one "coloured" for every 314 "coloured" inhabitants. I am not desirous of asking too much attention to this particular estimate, which is open to error, for the reason that, in the census reports, black and "coloured" people are classed together; but I feel bound to say that, upon showing this estimate to the superintendents of several convict establishments in the South, I have been invariably told that, whether exact or inexact, it might be accepted as expressive of the general truth. If, therefore, the products of miscegenation be short life and excessive tendency to disease and crime, is miscegenation, even supposing honourable and legal miscegenation to be possible, a desirable way out of the difficulty? I venture to think not. Honourable miscegenation, besides, is out of the question.

One other solution has been proposed. It is, however, too important and many-sided a scheme for me to deal with at the close of this already too lengthy chapter.

CHAPTER VI.

I HAVE attempted to show that the negro problem in the Southern States cannot be satisfactorily solved by the limitation of the suffrage, by the surrender of any portion of the country to the control of the black majority, by education of the coloured citizen, or by miscegenation of the races. The central point of the situation is the presence of the negro in the South. If he were not there, there would be no negro difficulty. The solution, therefore, that alone promises to be thoroughly effective is his removal. His mere dissemination throughout the Union would not be sufficient. No scheme of emigration from the South to the North and West can permanently benefit the negro or settle the race question. The "colour line" is, as has been repeatedly shown, even more clearly defined in the North than in the South. Everywhere in the South, for example, one may see black and white cab-drivers, though they do not love one another, plying indiscriminately for hire, black and white bricklayers working on the same buildings, black and white compositors setting up type at adjoining cases; but in most parts of the North things are different. There, with very few exceptions, the negro is not admitted to ordinary trade-union organisations; he is remorselessly "crowded out" from every occupation and employment; and his position is, upon the whole, worse than in Georgia or Louisiana. If the seven or eight millions of coloured people were to-morrow scattered equally over the States, the South, no doubt, would be relieved, but neither the North and West nor the negro would be better off. A more radical programme of removal must be adopted by any party that earnestly desires alike the welfare of the inferior stock and the final solution of the problem. There must be another exodus from Egypt, another restoration of the captive tribes.

In its bare outline the policy with which I am about to deal is not new. One of Thomas Jefferson's most prophetic utterances was:—" Nothing is more clearly written in the Book of Destiny than the emancipation of the blacks; and it is equally certain that the two races will never live in a state of equal freedom under the same Government, so insurmountable are the barriers which nature, habit, and opinion have established between them."

Jefferson, who died nearly forty years before emancipation became an accomplished fact, did not omit to prepare, so far as lay in his power, for the evil which he saw approaching. With Henry Clay and others, he founded the African Colonisation Society, which established on the west coast of Africa the Negro Republic of Liberia, and, between 1820 and 1860, sent thither about 10,000 free coloured people. It may at once be admitted that the colony has not been a conspicuous success, for the American immigrants and their descendants now hardly number 5,000 souls, and, according to Mr. Charles H. J. Taylor, a late American Minister to the Republic, the place is to-day " a land of snakes, centipedes, fever, miasma, poverty, superstition, and death." But the comparative failure of the Liberia scheme is due, in my humble opinion, rather to the principles in accordance with which it was carried out than to any inherent and necessary unfitness of the negro for colonisation. I shall later point out what appears to me to be the weak points in the Constitution of Liberia, as well as in that of Hayti. If they lie where I suspect they do, it is only natural that Jefferson and his associates and successors should have overlooked them.

Nor were Jefferson and his friends the only ones who, early in the century, sought to fend off the looming negro difficulty. In 1825 Senator Rufus King, of New York, was so far-seeing as to introduce to the United States Senate a resolution declaring that " the whole public land of the United States, with the net proceeds of all future sales thereof, shall constitute and form a fund which is hereby appropriated ; and the faith of the United States is hereby pledged that the said fund shall be inviolably applied to aid the emancipation of such slaves within any of the United States, and to aid the removal of such slaves and the removal of such free persons of colour in any of the United States, as by the laws of the States respectively shall be allowed to be emancipated, to any territory or country without the limits of the United States."

Senator King was far in advance of his day and generation, and, not unnaturally, his motion came to nothing ; but it is very likely indeed that, had it been carried, there would at the present moment be no considerable number of negroes in North America. The sum of money which under his scheme would already have become available for the removal of the coloured people exceeds £50,000,000 sterling, exclusive of interest, and the lands still undisposed of are worth, at a moderate computation, a hundred millions more.

Nothing practical, however, save the Liberia experiment, was attempted in Mr. King's day, or has been attempted since, towards the final solution of a problem which for a generation has been yearly growing graver and more dangerous.

It looks now as if the moment were about to arrive when either the question must be peaceably settled or it will settle itself by violence; and it is, therefore, worth while to consider whether the most radical and permanent solution of the difficulty is practicable, and, supposing it to be so, how it may, even at this late hour, be accomplished without force and injustice.

First, let me premise that the United States, as a whole, and not merely the South, owes an enormous debt to the negro race. Everyone admits that the institution of slavery was a crime against humanity; but everyone does not remember that for a century and more the North was *particeps criminis.* Some aspects of her responsibility will be found dealt with in the Appendix on Slavery in the North. It is too often forgotten that Southern slavery, up to the time of emancipation, existed under and was protected by the laws of the Union.

The debt owing to the blacks is manifold.

Something is due to those who, against their will, were dragged from their homes, subjected to the untold horrors of the middle passage, and forced to labour, unrequited, for strangers. What the horrors of the middle passage were is hinted at rather than told in the log-book of Her Majesty's ship *Skipjack*, which, in 1835, captured the Portuguese slaver *Martha*, with 447 slaves on board. The *Martha* had left Loango forty-three days before for Brazil with a freight of 790 slaves, of whom 353, or nearly 45 per cent., had perished from the tortures and miseries of the voyage. These tortures and miseries were not less, we may be sure, fifty or one hundred years earlier. Something, again, is due to those who, in the land of their captivity, were deprived by law of education, of the privilege of marriage, and of the guardianship of their children. More, per-haps, is due to those who, in support of the triumphant principles of the land of their captivity, shed their blood. As many as 300,000 people of colour took arms during the Civil War. And thankful recognition, if nothing beyond, is owing by the South to the subject race which, in the hour of national adversity, instead of rising to complicate the troubles of the Confederacy, was loyal, and even helpful, to the dominant class. There are other grounds of indebtedness, but they

have been so fully indicated in the course of this
work that I need not again specify them. My
only objects here are to insist upon the fact that
a heavy debt has been incurred, and to point
out that the time has not yet come when the
United States can say, " We are doing something
tangible towards paying it off."

In considering the practicability of the removal
from the United States of the blacks and coloured
people, one must bear in mind the following
questions :—

Is the negro willing to go ?

Can the negro be dispensed with ?

How can he be removed ?

Whither can he be sent ?

First let me attempt to offer a reply to the
question, " Is the negro willing to go ? " I believe
that he is, but he can best answer for himself.
The Rev. T. S. Lee, a coloured clergyman of
Charleston, speaking on Emancipation Day, 1890,
said :—

" I believe that the ultimate solution of the so-called race
problem will be emigration, from necessity, if not from choice.
. . . For two people so distinct from each other in their
physical structure, and between whom there are naturally
such insurmountable barriers, to develop on separate and
distinct lines, dwelling together here, is about as reasonable as
for two kings to reign on the same throne at one and the same
time. . . . We make a great mistake when we suppose

that the Anglo-Saxon gave us our enfranchisement for the love
he had for us . . . He did it because he thought he could
use us. . . . It is a mistaken idea for us to kneel down to
the whites. The Anglo-Saxon and the black man cannot work
together; one or the other will have to leave, and I am somewhat of a believer in the tale about the Lord's fire. The fire
will not burn the people, but it will be so warm that our
people will have to move on or get burnt; and I rather
believe that they will move on. . . . We must show our
independence, and the sooner we do this the better. Let some
of us leave—go to Africa if necessary—and show that we can
get along without the Anglo-Saxon, and, by this spirit of
independence, make him learn and appreciate our value.
Independence and emigration are, in my opinion, the only
solutions to this great question."

And Mr. Lee does not stand alone. Bishop
H. M. Turner, of Atlanta, Georgia, a leader
among the negro Methodists, said, in the course
of a public speech in 1889, that nothing but
poverty had kept his people where they were,
and that nothing but actual departure from the
country could cure existing evils.

And a few days later, he said, with reference
to the Morgan Bill which was then before Congress :—

"May God grant that the Bill may pass. The white people
brought us here against our will. Now they ought to provide
for us to leave if we desire. Besides, we must work out our
destiny anyhow, and if a portion of us think we can do it
better elsewhere, let the nation help us to try it. If the Bill

meant compulsory expatriation, we would fight it to the death; but, as it is voluntary upon the part of the negro, let it pass as soon as possible. The negro at best is but a scullion here, and he can be no less in Africa. I am tired of negro problems, lynch law, mob rule, and continual fuss, and millions of other negroes are tired of it. We want peace at some period in our existence, and if we cannot have it here, where we were born and reared, let that portion of us who choose to try another section of the world have a little help. This nation owes the negro forty billion of dollars any way ; so give us a little to emigrate upon."

Dr. Edward Wilmot Blyden, formerly of the West Indies and more recently of Sierra Leone, is another distinguished negro who advocates negro emigration from the States. More than this, in November, 1889, a negro colonisation society was established in Augusta, Georgia, to promote emigration to Africa. At about the same time a wholesale emigration of negroes to Mexico was projected, and a negro delegation visited the city of Mexico to make arrangements for it; while, a little earlier, a large scheme of negro migration from the States to the Argentine Republic was extensively advocated by most of the negro journals of the South. Unfortunately, neither Mexico nor the Argentine Republic wants the negro. The Mexican newspapers, as with one voice, bitterly attacked the scheme, and called upon their Government to be patriotic,

and not to countenance a plan which would bring
into the Republic a race alien in blood and
language. And the Buenos Ayres *Standard*
said:—" The darkey is destined to give the
United States far more trouble some day
than the detested heathen Chinee ; and it would
be really too cool of Jonathan to ask us here
to help him out of the unsavoury mess." The
Prensa, a Spanish newspaper of the same city,
declared upon the same occasion :—

> " It cannot be comprehended that a country proud, as ours
> is, of its wonderful and rapid advancement should commit the
> folly of introducing an element of obstruction, offensive both
> to sight and smell, and with marked tendencies to laziness.
> The United States would ridicule South America if the latter
> were to accept this Greek gift."

But these remarks do not touch the question of
the negro's readiness to migrate. There is really
no doubt that he is quite ready, provided always
that migration will better him, and provided also
that he can accomplish it without serious immediate loss to himself.

Can he, then, be spared ? The answer, I
think, is " Yes." The Birmingham, Alabama,
Age-Herald took up the question in June, 1889,
and thus expressed itself :—

> " In the lowlands of the Mississippi delta, the river bottoms
> of Arkansas and Louisiana, the Alabama black belt, and the

South Carolina coast, negro labour may seem indispensable ; but this is simply because the big plantation system exists in those sections. It would be a blessing to the South if the big plantation system could everywhere be broken up, and small farms, occupied and cultivated by thrifty white owners, substituted. In Texas, in Georgia—in all parts of the South, in fact, except those enumerated above—the white farmers work their own fields, and work them to much better advantage than those tenanted out to negroes. . . . The negro can be easily dispensed with, and if he stays in the South it is painful to conceive what must be the inevitable consequence. . . . The negro must go, or those Southern communities where he is found in such large numbers will go to something worse than perdition."

Upon this the Memphis *Avalanche* of June 8th, 1889, remarked :—

"We have no hesitation in endorsing as true everything the *Age-Herald* has said. There are hundreds and thousands of white labourers in the cotton fields of the South to-day. In Texas, where an immense amount of cotton is grown, a negro is frequently not seen in a day's ride."

The New Orleans *Times-Democrat*, one of the most respectable and influential of Southern journals, on June 17th, 1889, took the same view in very decided terms, and added :—

"There is no portion of the South where the whites cannot live, where they do not work more intelligently and better than the negroes, and where they do not produce larger crops *per capita*. The South would be more productive, richer, and more prosperous in every way if it were peopled altogether by white men."

The Galveston, Texas, *News* held similar language ; so did the Charleston *News and Courier ;* so did the Atlanta *Constitution*, the Nashville *American*, the Richmond *Dispatch*, the Arkansas *Democrat*, the New Orleans *Picayune*, and, in brief, all the leading newspapers of the South. Indeed, I know of no important exception. Concerning the filling of the gap which would be created by the removal of the negro, the Greenville, South Carolina, *News* of March 17th, 1889, had already said :—

" If we can keep the white people there will be no lack of labour and population. The natural increase may be trusted to occupy every acre of available ground without the coming of new citizens ; but we might reasonably hope for a great inflow of white immigration to follow the tide of coloured emigration."

Colonel Stokes, a representative Southern, writing on the same subject, argues forcibly and convincingly against the assumption that the negro is an essential element in cotton raising. " It is generally admitted by all who are acquainted with the matter that the negroes are the most inefficient of all labourers in nearly all the fields of labour. The Southern negroes cultivate an average of not more than six or eight acres to the hand ; the Northern farmer cultivates forty to sixty acres. The latter uses a great variety of improved farming implements. The negro cannot be taught to use any other than the primitive types he has been long accustomed to. Still, the planter is dependent upon the negro to till his fields simply because the negro is here and cannot be got rid of, and white labour is not available in any sufficient numbers while the field is so occupied. But it is certain that if the negro cotton-raiser could everywhere be replaced by white men, the cotton region would wear a very different aspect."

There are even signs that the negro is being dispensed with already, and that, if he remain, his position as a labourer will deteriorate rather than improve. The *Forum* for December, 1889, contained a powerful article on " The Race Problem," by Professor Scomp, of Emory College, Georgia. The writer, in summing up, says :—

" Sadly, yet with perfect conviction, we are driven to the inevitable conclusion that if the negro's citizenship and his social and business privileges are to have play and development, it must be upon another soil than that of the whites. As equals, the races cannot and will not exist together."

And, writing privately to Dr. E. W. Blyden, Professor Scomp thus explains his views as to one aspect of the negro's future in the States :—

" One feature which I regard as ominous to the future of most of the Southern negroes is the steady and rapid improve-

N

ment in machinery in all departments of the cotton-plantation industry ; *e.g.*, less than two months ago there was exhibited at the Georgia State Fair, at Macon, a machine for chopping cotton, by which one man, upon a kind of buggy plough, could in one day do the work, by horse-power, of more than a dozen ordinary choppers. Such machinery, generally introduced, must, for the most part, put an end to the plantation negro's summer work and his means of subsistence. Many efforts, too, are making at the invention of a proper cotton-picking machine, and, though this has not yet succeeded to any great degree, American industry will undoubtedly prove equal to the task of invention. When that day comes the mass of Southern negroes will be practically out of an occupation and without a livelihood."

Apart from this, the negro is now doing much less in the South than he used to do. The Charleston *News and Courier*, which made a careful investigation of this matter in South Carolina, county by county, a few years ago, found that 30 per cent. of the cotton was raised by white and 70 per cent. by coloured labour. In Mississippi the State census of 1880, taken coincidentally with the United States census, showed that 328,568 bales were produced by white and 627,240 bales by negro labour. In these States, with large negro majorities, nearly a third of the cotton crop was raised by the whites. Judging by these figures, it is safe to say that, including the comparatively white States of Texas and Arkansas, very nearly half the cotton is raised by the whites, whereas thirty years ago not over 400,000 bales, or one-tenth the crop, was grown by them.

If, as would appear to be the case, the negro be willing to migrate and can be dispensed with, the next questions for consideration are—How can he be removed? And whither can he be sent? The two questions are intimately allied, and may best be examined together. I think that a rough key to one of them has been furnished by Mr. J. A. D. Mitchell, who, writing on January 11th, 1890, to the Cleveland, Ohio, *Gazette*, a newspaper conducted by and in the interests of coloured people, says:—

"Let the United States Government assume a protectorate over such portions of the African Continent as are not already provided for, and, to enforce the claim, call for 100,000 or more American negro volunteers to assist, not only in the abolition of the slave traffic, but also in Christianising and reclaiming the African negro from heathenism and idolatry. I claim that climatic and other influences preclude the possibility of the white man accomplishing much without the aid and influence of the negro. . . . The necessity for forced emigration or colonisation would (either being distasteful as well as impracticable) be supplanted by a voluntary uprising of the negro to participate in reclaiming the land of his forefathers."

There is here, I really believe, the germ, though only the germ, of a sound and useful

N 2

scheme. It is not likely that the United States Government will, in our day, assume onerous protectorates in other continents; and it is not, I am convinced, desirable that, in the future home of the negro, the emigrant shall live under institutions similar to those which at present contribute so much to his discomfort. If the black were to move to what would practically be an American foreign possession, he would scarcely improve his position. He would still find himself on nominal equality with, but in actual inferiority to, the white governing powers. If not, he would have to govern himself; and for this task the negro is peculiarly unfitted. It is for this reason that Hayti and Liberia have proved failures.

Where I detect the true ring in Mr. Mitchell's crude suggestion is in his proposal that the negro shall be given not only a country, but also a stimulus to make himself worthy of the boon. In one or other of these, to my mind, absolutely essential features, all the remaining projects of negro migration that have come under my notice are lacking.

Several Bills, aspiring to deal in an adequate manner with the race problem, have lately been brought before the notice of the United States Senate. Senator Butler, of South Carolina, asked for the appropriation of five millions of dollars

in aid of negro emigration generally. Senator
Gibson, of Louisiana, advocated the acquirement,
as the negro's future home, of extra-Union territory. Senator Morgan, of Alabama, brought
forward a scheme of African colonisation; and
Senator Call, of Florida, revived the old project of opening negotiations with Spain to secure the establishment in Cuba of a negro
republic.

But all these legislators have missed the one
important point. You cannot, without the use of
force, ensure anything approaching to a general
exodus of a whole race, unless you first provide
the people with high aims, and also hold out to
them a reasonable hope of improved political,
social, and financial conditions. Had the Israelites seen nothing better than Egypt before them,
they would never have quitted the land of
Goshen; had the Babylonian captives not looked
to the rebuilding of the Temple, it is doubtful
whether many of them would have availed themselves of Cyrus's permission to return to
Palestine.

Speaking in the Senate on the subject of the
Butler Bill, Senator Wade Hampton, who has
been one of the most honoured and successful
Governors of South Carolina, the blackest State
in the Union, said, on January 30th, 1890:—

"I have expressed the opinion that the separation of the white and coloured races in the United States would be of permanent benefit to both. . . . I recognise as fully as anyone the political rights of the coloured people, and amongst these rights is that paramount one of every citizen of the Republic to choose his own home. The forcible expulsion of the negroes would not only be unlawful, but would be impolitic, unjust and cruel. . . . No thoughtful patriotic man would contemplate any such action. But whilst patriotism, wisdom, and an enlarged philanthropy dictate these views, it may still be a question whether some feasible plan cannot be adopted by which such coloured people as desire to seek a new home, where, under their own laws and their own government, they could work out their own destiny free from contact with the white race, could not receive the generous and fostering assistance of this great and rich Government."

Like his brother legislators, Senator Hampton fails to grasp the necessity of giving to the negroes a motive to induce them to leave the States; like them, too, he appears to be of opinion that, no matter whither the negro may remove, he must be, if not an American subject, at least a self-governing individual. On both these points, I venture to think, his attitude is a wrong one; but on the other point which is dealt with in this extract from his speech he is right. The American Government ought, in recognition of its indebtedness, as well as from politic consideration of its own best interests, to be prepared to assist the proposed negro emigration; and on that point Senators Butler, Gibson, Morgan, and Call are in practical agreement with Senator Hampton.

One of the most conspicuous characteristics of the negro is, as I have already had occasion to point out, his childishness. Referring to the negroes of Africa, Mr. H. M. Stanley, writing in December last to *The Times*, said :—

"If one regards these natives as mere brutes, then the annoyances that their follies and vices inflict are, indeed, intolerable. In order to rule them and to keep one's life amongst them, it is needful resolutely to regard them as children, who require, indeed, different methods of rule from English or American citizens, but who must be ruled in precisely the same spirit, with the same absence of caprice and anger, the same essential respect to our fellow-men."

Another recent writer has said of them :— "They are children; children naughty or children good; pleased or angry; children to be ruled firmly, treated kindly; but always, at bottom, children." And everyone who knows thoroughly the African negro, either in Africa or in America, can have no other estimate of his character.

This being so, is it reasonable, on the one hand, to elevate the negro, as he has been elevated in America, to a level of political and legal equality with the Caucasian; or, on the other hand, to expect this child of nature to properly govern himself? The experiment of equality has failed in America; the experiment of self-government has failed in Hayti, in Liberia, and wherever else it has been tried. Surely, then, it is as necessary, in the experiment of the future, to avoid placing the negro on a pedestal which he has proved himself incapable of occupying as it is to avoid enslaving him, oppressing him, or in any way unfairly treating him. If my contentions be sound, it results that the experiment of the future must be conducted with due regard to the following conditions :—

1. The emigrating negro must be offered a country in which he may pursue high aims, enjoy a prospect of improved political, social, and financial *status*, and find climate and employment suited to his needs.

2. He must not govern, but be governed. At the same time he must not be oppressed, either physically or morally; and there must be no restraint upon his improvement and advancement.

3. His emigration must be assisted, either by those who owe him a debt or by those who will benefit by his migration, or by both.

Accepting the above conditions as postulates, I may now definitely indicate what, after a long and careful study of the problem in its various aspects, seems to be the only solution that will be alike just and permanent.

The country that is most suitable for the negro is, beyond all cavil, that central belt of Africa which lies between the Sahara and the Tropic of Capricorn, and which includes the Congo Free State, Senegambia, Liberia, the British and German possessions on the Gulf of Guinea, Sierra Leone, Gaboon, Angola, Damaraland, Mozambique, Zanzibar, and the territories of the various British and German African companies. The greater part of this belt is the negro's own country, the place whence his ancestors were kidnapped, or in which his race still dwells; and, so far as civilisation is concerned, nearly all of it is, to this day, virgin soil.

The past fifty years have witnessed the first serious attempts on the part of civilisation to open up this immense district, the riches and fertility of which no one, even now, is in a position to estimate. Very little progress has been made. The climate and general conditions are, over much of the tract, unsuitable for the majority of Europeans. European influences, nevertheless, are almost everywhere dominant; and almost everywhere there exists the framework, though not all the machinery, of just government. The crying need of the situation is more civilisation—civilisation not of a very advanced or cultured variety, but rather civilisation of a kind which, not being too much superior to native habits and modes of thought, and being, nevertheless, of a moderately progressive type, may first, if properly encouraged and led by white influence, capture the Africans and then gradually raise them with itself to higher planes.

Who are more suited to apply such modest civilisation to the blacks of Africa than the blacks of America? Africa, as a whole, will never be a white man's country. It will not, therefore, be the scene of such race jealousies as torment the Southern States of the American Union.

At the same time, Africa, it is tolerably certain, will always have the advantage of white rule, and of a kind of white rule, moreover, that will not possess the irksome defects of white rule as it now exists in America. In no British colony, for example, is there any reason why a capable negro should not raise himself to high position and honour. In no British colony, on the other hand, does the negro govern. And I think it may also be said that in every British colony in which he is to be found the negro is a fairly happy and contented person. It is a great mistake to suppose, as many people do, that the negro objects to be governed, and to be governed firmly. On the contrary, he likes it, provided always that the government be fair as well as firm. Colonel Shepard, an acknowledged advocate of the negro, admits, with regard to the present condition of Hayti, that the whole business is a fine illustration of the futility of introducing republican institutions to a country whose people are uneducated, untrained in affairs, and incapable of self-government.

Nor is the negro hopelessly enamoured of the suffrage. He clings to it in the United States, because there it constitutes almost his only badge of humanity; but to those who will freely concede his humanity he will as freely surrender the suffrage.

By a wholesale migration, and properly conducted, of Southern negroes to Africa, America would be relieved, and Africa would be benefited.

Already this fact has, to a limited extent, been recognised and acted upon. In 1884 a plan for the introduction of Southern negro labour to the Congo district was submitted to the King of the Belgians by an American, Colonel George W. Williams; and I believe I am correct in saying that Colonel Williams was in consequence empowered to engage twelve clerks, accountants, and storekeepers at 125f. a month, and twelve mechanics and engineers at from 200f. to 300f. a month, transportation, board, lodging, and medical attendance to be provided by the Congo Free State. Five years later, in 1889, the King of the Belgians made application to the United States for twenty-four professional men and artisans to go to the Congo as representatives of the trained and educated American negro. His Majesty's agent visited, among other places, Shaw University, at Raleigh, North Carolina, a remarkably well-conducted college for coloured students. The principal, Dr. H. M. Tupper, declared his firm belief that thousands of American negroes would, within a few years, go to the Congo country ; and he said that he recognised in the opportunity a grand means of permanently improving the condition of many coloured people.

If the American negro were shown, as he easily might be shown, first, that his exodus to Africa would result in vast good to his race, and would open to him an honourable mission as a civiliser; next, that the proceeding would result in a general amelioration of his own condition; and finally, that in Africa he would escape from the discomforts and persecutions that hem in his career in America ; and if, at the same time, he were offered aid to enable him to migrate to and establish himself on the soil of his fathers, I do not doubt that he would leave America, not merely in his thousands, but in his millions. He desires, above all things, a country and an aim in life. Give him those, and he will seize them gladly. But it is useless to counsel him to go to Africa, or elsewhere, unless you also hold out to him an object to be attained. And even a grand object will not alone induce him to move. He is, as a rule, poor. His investments, such as they are, are all in America. It is necessary not only to assist him to move and settle, but also to pay him generously for the little that he must surrender.

It is impossible, while considering this scheme, to avoid thinking, again and again, of the parallelism of the exodus of the Israelites, and of the Biblical conclusion, "And they spoiled the Egyptians." The Egyptians, like the Americans, had incurred a great debt to their bondsmen, and, like the Americans, they sought to evade it, and suffered bitterly in consequence. But the payment was inevitable in Goshen, and it is inevitable in the United States. In Goshen it was paid in the form of spoils, surrendered in panic by a people who, at the last, were glad to be rid of their captives at any cost. How will it be paid in America ?

One cannot foresee, but it is quite certain that it is not yet too late for it to be voluntarily tendered in cold blood, and to be gratefully accepted; and it is reasonable to suppose that delay in payment will not lessen but rather increase the amount—be it of treasure, blood, misery, or unrest—to be ultimately paid.

It would seem, therefore, that principles of ordinary economy, as well as of common justice, indicate that an effort should be made to pay off the negro as soon as possible.

It cannot be said that the Union has any lack of means. Her actual indebtedness at the conclusion of the Civil War was, roughly speaking, £551,286,000; it is now only £187,115,000, and between June 30th and October 1st, 1890, it was reduced by £14,537,000. In twenty-five years the Federal Debt has been lessened by £364,171,000, or at the average rate of over fourteen and a half millions sterling per annum; and the annual surplus available for reduction is now, as a rule, so much larger than it was a few years ago, while the debt remaining is of such very manageable proportions, that very little hardship to the United States would result from a temporary diversion—say, for thirty years—of a portion of the surplus from the purposes of the reduction of the Federal Debt to the payment of interest and gradual payment of principal of a special series of negro emigration and settlement loans.

It is calculated that an annual sum of twelve or fourteen millions sterling might thus, without undue pinching, be diverted; and this represents a very large capital amount—an amount which would probably be quite sufficient, with a certain quota of aid from outside, not only to decently transport, but to comfortably establish in Africa, every pure-blooded negro now on United States territory.

It might not be also sufficient to buy out the negro; but that might justly be assigned as a duty, in whole or in part, to the individual States concerned, seeing that they are more immediately interested than is the nation at large in getting rid of him, and that the expenditure to be incurred would sooner or later be returned to the States in the shape of payments on the re-sale of lands and buildings now belonging to the negroes.

That the United States have not already entered upon some such course is rather remarkable; for they have spent scores of millions in the payment of debts which are less pressing, and they have, indeed, been so generous in certain directions as to have incurred the reproach of unwarrantable extravagance. They have over half a million names on their pension-roll, and they pay the pensioners more than twenty millions a year, in spite of the fact that most of the persons who benefit had no legal claim upon the country at the time when the services in respect of which pensions are now paid were rendered. The pensions are not, as pensions are in England, deferred pay; they are compensations and gratuities. The Union has been lavish with them; but the Governments which have granted them have always looked forward to a return in the shape of political support, and so the sums disbursed have been regarded as profitable in-vestments.

Hitherto, there is no doubt, American politicians as a body have not discovered that any profit can result from the payment of the nation's indebtedness to the negro; and that is the reason why they have not dealt with the negro as they have dealt with the soldier.

But will there be no profit? The South is now stagnant under the incubus of the negro.

According to Governor Lee, of Virginia, the negro does not " pay " as a citizen. The Greenville *News* goes so far as to make the following estimate of the results which would follow upon the removal of two-thirds of the present coloured population from South Carolina:—

" We should lose," it says, " $50,000 to $75,000, which is probably a full estimate of the total amount of taxes paid by coloured people; the cultivation of some land, the production of some cotton, for a time. We should have about $175,000 of the amount now used for coloured public schools for the use of white schools, nearly doubling the present terms and adding much to the facilities and comforts of teachers and scholars. We should have in the penitentiary about 100 convicts instead of 800. Our criminal courts would sit on an average from a day to a day and a half a week, nine-tenths of their time being now occupied by trying coloured persons. Our gaols would have about one-fifth of the inmates they now have, nineteen-twentieths of the prisoners now fed and kept at the cost of the taxpayers being coloured. The lunatic asylum would have one-half its present population and would cost one-half of what it now costs. The county poor-houses would contain one-half, or less, of their present population. The trial justices would have, on an average, about a case a month. These calculations are from the actual figures. What we should gain in the way of keeping white people who are now crowded out by coloured competition, the improvement of lands by intelligent and careful cultivation, and the incoming of white mechanics and farmers, are matters of further estimation."

The Union is divided, and it is the presence of the negro that causes the division. Nearly one-eighth of the population of the Union is of alien race, and, besides being hopelessly alien, is oppressed, discontented, and dangerous. These are evils which might be abolished to the general profit. And worse evils lurk in the future. The prosecution of a race war would not be cheaper than the promotion of a negro exodus. The severance from the Union of six or eight States

O

would be vastly more weakening to the nation as a whole. In some form the debt must be paid. Nature has never yet admitted the plea of any Statute of Limitations in cases like the one under discussion. It were well, then, to make a settlement while it can still be made peacefully and, comparatively speaking, cheaply.

If America would do its duty by the negro, those civilised nations which have established themselves in Africa would, in pursuance of their own interests, aid her. Great Britain, Germany, and France would each and all welcome the immigration to their African possessions of large and leavening bodies of American blacks. Not long ago Sir Alfred Moloney, Governor of Lagos, received a deputation from "the Brazilian and Havannah repatriates in the colony of Lagos," and was assured that all the negroes of Brazil wished to return to the country of their ancestors. In reply, Sir Alfred Moloney said that he had induced the commercial world to take an interest in the project, and that the African Steamship Company had engaged to provide improved and cheaper facilities for negro immigrants from Brazil. He welcomed the idea of "repatriation," and would encourage it. Much more, no doubt, would he welcome the idea of the "repatriation" of the immeasurably more civilised and less debauched American negro. The black, it is true, will not do much good for himself anywhere without white superintendence, but there is no reason why such superintendence as is necessary should not be forthcoming, and, if it be once understood that the salvation of Africa lies with the negro even more than with the white, there is every ground for believing that the American negro will rise bravely to the occasion.

Even in a greater degree than in the African possessions of Great Britain, Germany, and France does there appear to be a career for the American negro in the Congo Free State. The author of "An Appeal to Pharaoh" has indicated that State as the American negro's promised land. A copy of the book was recently given to Mr. H. M. Stanley, a man who, having spent parts of his life not only in the Dark Continent but also in Louisiana, knows the negro both in America and in Africa. The volume drew from the traveller a very interesting letter, from which I extract the following:—.

"There is space enough in one section of the Upper Congo basin to locate double the number of the negroes of the United States without disturbing a single tribe of the aborigines now inhabiting it. I refer to the immense Upper Congo forest country, 350,000 square miles in extent, which is three times larger than the Argentine Republic, and one and a half times larger than the entire German Empire, embracing

o 2

224,000,000 acres of umbrageous forest land, wherein every
unit of the 7,000,000 negroes might become the owner of
nearly a quarter square mile of land. Five acres of this,
planted with bananas and plantains, would furnish every soul
with sufficient subsistence—food and wine. The remaining
twenty-seven acres of his estate would furnish him with timber,
rubber, gums, dye-stuffs, for sale. There are 150 days of rain
throughout the year. There is a clear stream every few
hundred yards. In a day's journey we have crossed as many
as thirty-two streams. The climate is healthy and equable,
owing to the impervious forest which protects the land from
chilly winds and draughts. All my white officers passed
through the wide area safely. Eight navigable rivers course
through it. Hills and ridges diversify the scenery and give
magnificent prospects. To those negroes in the South accustomed to Arkansas, Mississippi, and Louisiana, it would be a
reminder of their own plantations without the swamps and the
depressing influence of cypress forests. Anything and everything might be grown in it, from the oranges, guavas, sugar-
cane, and cotton of sub-tropical lands to the wheat of California
and the rice of South Carolina. If the emigration were
prudently conceived and carried out, the glowing accounts sent
home by the first settlers would soon dissipate all fear and
reluctance on the part of the others. But it is all a dream.
The American capitalists, like other leaders of men, are more
engaged in decorating their wives with diamonds than in
busying themselves with national questions of such import as
removing the barrier between the North and the South. The
' open sore ' of America—the race question—will ever remain
an incurable fester. While we are all convinced that the
Nessus shirt which clings to the Republic has maddened her,
and may madden her again, it is quite certain that the
small effort needed to free themselves for ever from it will
never be made."

I am inclined to be more sanguine than Mr. Stanley was when he wrote that letter. Some solution of the race question cannot be long deferred, and surely there is enough latent justice and prudence in the American people to induce them to render the inevitable solution a peaceable and equitable one.

In a still later utterance on the subject Mr. Stanley has taken a cheerier view. The Congo Government, he declares, is favourable, and the laws are calculated to promote happiness and content. Whites cannot colonise the State, since a white man living in the Congo Valley for three years expends ten years of vitality, while women cannot retain health.

" With negroes forming the majority of its citizenship, the State would, with proper encouragement, make remarkable development, and, in time, become a great nation. . . . At present the Congo Free State's government is entirely in the hands of whites, but, in my opinion, any man who can prove his capacity would receive all that any could expect."

For the half-breed of the South another haven must be sought. He is no more the friend of the black than he is of the white. Neither desires his company. But in the West Indies, or in some parts of South and Central America, he might, no doubt, discover a land in which his existence would be a not unpleasant one.

I have discussed this great subject copiously, but very inadequately. No question at present before the world has so many aspects; and to America no question is equally important. The solution which I have advocated is costly; but it is, I believe, the only one that promises a permanent and honourable settlement of the difficulty. Any other must be imperfect, or must involve wholesale bloodshed. Until something of the kind is put into practice, the dearly bought union must remain a nominal one, and North and South must continue to cherish different aims, and to be, in effect, separate nations. Only when the negro shall have departed will the name of the United States truly represent anything more than a magnificent aspiration.

It would be ungenerous to conclude this work without some acknowledgment of the great assistance that has been rendered to me in my study of the subject by, among others, Mr. Eustace Ballard Smith, Mr. John Bigelow, Mr. P. Bigelow, Major Post, U.S.A., Mr. Chauncey M. Depew, Mr. J. W. Barnwell, Mr. G. W. Cable, Mr. Theodore Roosevelt, Mr. C. M'Kinley, Mr. S. J. E. Rawling, Mr. R. W. Gilder, and the Governors of most of the Southern States. To them, and to many others, including a number of negro gentlemen, whose names, if I have not already mentioned them incidentally, are, at their own wish, withheld, I desire to express my most grateful thanks, coupled with the sincere hope that the difficulty which interests all of them, and which is only fortunate in that it has enabled me to make their acquaintance, may, before long, cease to exist.

APPENDIX.

A.—THE POPULATION OF THE SOUTH IN 1890.

Up to the time of sending this book to the press, no official statistics of the relative proportions of the races in the Southern States of the Black Belt in 1890 have reached me from Washington. Bulletin No. 16 of the Census Office contains, however, a final statement as to the total population of each State in question. I give the figures in tabular form, leaving vacant columns for the insertion hereafter of the missing information :—

	Total Population, 1890.	White.	Coloured.
North Carolina	1,617,947		
Virginia	1,655,980		
Georgia	1,837,353		
Florida	391,422		
Alabama	1,513,017		
Louisiana	1,118,587		
Mississippi	1,289,600		
South Carolina	1,151,149		
	10,575,055		

B.—COLOUR CASTE.

To the *Forum* for October, 1889 (*Forum* Publishing Company, 253, Fifth Avenue, New York), the Rev. John Snyder contributed an article with the above title. As it illustrates many points that are briefly touched upon in the present volume, I venture to append some further portions of it beyond those already quoted.

"A gifted American actor," says Mr. Snyder, "has conceived a professional scheme which promises an affluent return of profit and reputation. He is convinced that, under certain clearly recognised conditions, the drama of *Othello* may be made popular in the Southern States. He sees clearly, of course, why this great product of the master's genius has been 'under a cloud,' so to speak, south of Mason and Dixon's line, and he purposes revealing to the art-loving people of that section the beauties of a work which the interpretative power of the greatest actors of the past has never made tolerable on the Southern stage.

"He is conscious of the natural difficulties to be over-come ; of the state of social feeling which will always resent the intrusion of the African on the histrionic stage, except within the limited range of the minstrel show. But his system contemplates an easy solution of these apparently insuperable difficulties. He does not design to impart a less pronounced colour to the face of *Othello*, because experience has taught him that the slightest tinge of creaminess in the complexion and the faintest crinkle in the hair would leave the prejudice against his hero's race practically unaffected. He simply intends to 'improve' Shakspeare so that the great bard's creations may be made generally acceptable to all sections of our free and enlightened land.

"There is no intention wilfully to misrepresent Shakspeare,

or to distort his plain meanings. But this artist has reasoned
himself into the conviction that the great author's hero could
not have been a negro. Therefore, all the prejudice against
him on that ground is manifestly unreasonable. In the very
nature of things, he must have been the representative of
another race, or else *Brabantio's* friendship, *Desdemona's* love,
Cassio's esteem, and the unstinted admiration of Venice would
all be impossible and inconceivable. Accordingly, our actor
holds, *Othello* must have resembled one of those stately Arab
chiefs whose portraits gleam from the pages of ' Picturesque
Palestine.'

" Our Southern brethren are at last to have an *Othello* who
cannot, as the moral circus advertisements say, ' offend the
most fastidious.' Shakspeare, carefully modernised, will become popular once more in the sunny South. All references
to the blackness of *Othello's* face and the thickness of his lips
are to be conscientiously softened down into less objectionable
phrases, and those audiences which may be ethnologically
unenlightened are to have their sensitive natures soothed by
some such prologue as *Bottom* proposed for the sapient actors
of Athens : ' Ladies, or fair ladies, I would wish you, or I
entreat you, not to fear, not to tremble ; my life for yours. If
you think I come hither as a " nigger," it were a pity of my
life. I am no such thing. I am an Arab.' That would put
all doubt at rest.

" The only thing likely to interfere with the success of this
scheme of mingled philanthropy and profit is the presence of
that vast amount of astute Shakspearean philosophy which is
based upon the assumption of *Othello's* objectionable ethnic
relationship. What becomes of Professor D. J. Snider's
' System of Shakspeare's Dramas.'? It is quite probable that
Shakspeare, could he be consulted, would offer no strenuous
objection to the proposed change. Having been an actor himself, he would doubtless sympathise with the despair to which

the modern representative of his profession is reduced in the task of catering to the present unreasonable demand for dramatic novelties. As there is not the slightest appreciable trace of a 'system' in any of his dramas, and as the social prejudice against the African race as such is something which in his day and generation was still unborn, it is reasonable to suppose that *Othello* might be re-made into a Chinaman or a Choctaw without seriously affecting the motive of the tragedy.

"Still, when a man has constructed a 'System of Shakspeare,' and has announced that 'Shakspeare makes race an ethical element of marriage, as important as chastity,' and that 'in Europe to-day the marriage of a lord and a servant-girl collides with the moral consciousness of the whole public,' he naturally has the same kind of affection for that system which Dr. Sangrado had for his, and any attempt to upset its 'ethical' conclusions by substituting an Arabian *Othello* for an Ethiopian, will be apt to be resented. It is as fundamentally unethical to marry an Arab as a negro. It will be much wiser for our actor frankly to retain the African characteristics of his hero, letting it be understood that a true Shakspearean system employs this tragedy as an 'awful example' to warn those who are tempted to leap over the ethical fence of racial distinctions.

"Once outside of the atmosphere of American social life, it is difficult to treat the spirit of colour caste with seriousness or decent respect. Of course, that man would be but a shallow ethnologist who should maintain that the terms 'superior' and 'inferior' do not justly mark the distinctions between races, or who should refuse to acknowledge that certain choice characteristics of civilisation are confined within fairly well-ascertained racial limitations. And the man who looks with disapproval upon marriage unions between the members of a progressive race like the Caucasian, and the members of a conditionally unimprovable race, is governed by principles of

the simplest prudence, to say no more. The difficulty is always
in determining this question of improvability. The Spanish
race in its various colonies has seemed to stand still for three
centuries, yet to attribute racial inferiority to the countrymen
of Cervantes and Loyola would be manifestly unjust. The
negro race in this country may be mentally and morally both
inferior and unimprovable, and hence it would be both wise
and ethical for our stock to refuse to make with it a mixture
of blood. But the average American knows nothing and
cares nothing about any physiological reasons for declining
such marriages. In truth, the race question does not, with
us, involve this marriage element at all. Generally speaking,
nobody wants his daughter to marry a negro, and the negro is
not anxious to seek such marriages. As a matter of fact, in
the matter of marriage the negro is ridiculously fastidious,
accepting without complaint the white man's classification of
every shade of colour, even the slightest, under the head of
negro, and rigorously claiming for his own race every possible
modification of the original type. There are plenty of octoroons
and quadroons who might easily pass for members of the white
race, but who never think of seeking marriage associations
outside their mother's stock. And they would be subjected to
the severe censure of the black race if they did so. The
bugbear of 'miscegenation' is the least substantial phantom
that haunts the imagination of ignorant people.

"The cruel wall of caste which has been relentlessly built
around the negro in this country was not created by the fear
of racial deterioration on the part of the Caucasian. The feeling
from which it sprang is so inexplicable as almost to defy any
philosophical analysis. That in the Southern States slavery
should have created a clearly defined colour caste was reasonable and natural. That among a people generous in disposition
and generally religious in their habits of mind this caste
feeling should have been strengthened by every argument

tending to show the negro's natural inferiority and fitness for his servile position was equally natural. That within the limits of slave territory every Southern gentleman should con- sider the presence of mental ability in an individual negro a reflection upon the system and a menace to its continuance, was the most reasonable thing in the world. But it is only justice to say that not in the South but in the North did this curious feeling of colour caste first have its rise. The Southern man apparently denied to the negro social recognition not primarily because he was a negro, but because he was a slave. The Northern man seems to hate the negro primarily on account of his colour. In domestic service, the filthiest and most ignorant Irish or German servant refuses to eat at the same table with the cleanest and most respectable negro. In some of our hotels the wealthiest negro in the land could not purchase, at any price, the privilege of sitting in the common dining room, or of occupying one of the sleeping apartments. Industrially, he is practically restricted to a "beggarly account," of the least profitable and most menial trades. Those labour unions which complain so bitterly of the oppression of capital, and announce Utopian principles of universal brotherhood, do not dare to cast their mantle of protection over the despised and neglected labourer with a black skin. But saddest of all is the attitude which the Church has held towards this spirit of colour caste. Ideally, at least, the Church is the home of human equality. All classes and conditions of men are supposed to meet there on a common ground. And while we constantly depart from this principle in practice, we usually try to cover and disguise our shortcomings by a thin veil of self-exculpation. We may not want the poor and poorly dressed man sitting in our pews, but we rarely make a frank confession of the fact. Only the negro is openly, and by common consent, excluded from the broad definition of Christian equality. We have not yet accepted Mr. Nasby's advice, and altered our version of the New Testament so that it shall read 'Suffer the little (white) children to come unto Me,' but it would be quite consistent for us to do so.

"This condition of things would cease to be mysterious if it were based upon recognised physiological reasons. We can easily understand *Brabantio's* surprise when his daughter became enamoured of a thick-lipped African, or Aunt Ophelia's disgust at seeing Eva hanging about the neck of Uncle Tom. We are not disposed to question the good Puritan's conviction that the pure negro is 'an acquired taste.' But we entertain the same personal and social repugnance for every possible modification of the negro. Even when the bleaching process has been so thorough that no external indication of African blood remains; even when the individual has assumed all the characteristics of Caucasian beauty and intelligence, we still treat him as a social pariah. Several years ago there was, at a certain school in Pittsburg, a very beautiful and intelligent young lady. In scholarship and deportment she stood for a year at the head of the school. At the end of that time somebody told the principal that his favourite pupil had lurking in her veins a few unsuspected and undiscoverable drops of African blood. She was turned out of the doors as ignominiously as if she had been guilty of unchastity or was afflicted with some infectious disease.

"Tell the average American that he is descended from Pocahontas, that his blood may be traced to Confucius, or that his daughter has secretly married one of Madame Blavatsky's mythical Indian Mahatmas, and the chances are that he will be flattered and gratified. You stumble over no 'ethical principle'; you encounter no fatal racial prejudice. Tell him that his great-great-grandfather was probably a powerful potentate from the Congo or the Niger, and you touch the acme of insult. It would be safer to accuse him of highway robbery.

" But the most astonishing feature of this colour caste is found in the complacent assumption of the average American that it is something inherent and natural in the human mind, and is therefore universal. Tell such a person that it is the result of social and political education, and he will smile at your ignorance. Yet when such an American steps over the borders of his own country he does not find this prejudice shared by any other nation. The Frenchman, Englishman, or German may not want his daughter to marry a negro, but in no part of Europe do you detect the presence of that galling system of social discrimination which so exasperates the black man in this country. All over the continent of Europe you find the negro living in the best hotels, travelling in first class coaches, and sitting as an equal on the benches of the great scientific and art schools. You find no trace of this prejudice in the press or literature of Europe; you find no taint of it in its social life. London is the great meeting-place of all the varied races of the world. A new Peter would find there the representatives of more peoples than listened to the many-tongued sermon on the Day of Pentecost. All colours and conditions of men make up the varied web and woof of its marvellous life. Each man's condition is determined by his rank, his wealth, his social position. Social caste indeed exists of the most rigid type ; but it is never based on colour, hardly ever upon racial distinctions. It may be, as the author of the ' System of Shakspeare's Dramas ' affirms, that the marriage of a lord and a servant-girl ' collides with the moral conscious-ness of the whole public,' but a man's treatment is conditioned upon his wealth, his intelligence, his knowledge, his rank, or his personal character, never upon the colour of his skin. In the light of this fact our colour caste seems as provincial as it is undeniably absurd, cruel, and indefensible."

C.—SLAVERY IN THE NORTH.

The following letter was addressed in 1888 to the Editor of, and was printed in, the Charleston *News and Courier*. As it deals very ably, though from a pronouncedly Southern standpoint, with the responsibility of the North towards the negro, I reprint it with a few insignificant corrections :—

"Sir,—I was glad to see your editorial on March 9th last on the Emancipation Proclamation. It is surprising how much ignorance exists upon the subject of emancipation in some of the usually best-informed circles. I desire to call your attention to two instances of this in that usually accurate journal, the *Nation* (of New York). In a recent number there appeared the review of a letter written from Washington to a paper in Frankfort :—

" ' The condition of our negro population is the subject of a Washington letter in the *Frankfurter Zeitung* of December 24th, 1887. The writer's view of their social status is correct enough, but he is rather at sea in his historical retrospect, as when he says that the South was at one time more opposed to slavery than was the North, and that the Civil War was a struggle between " the sons of the slave-owners and the planters to whom their fathers had sold their dark commodities." This is a corollary to the misleading statement that " in 1790 the negroes were distributed throughout this country, and were almost exclusively slaves," but that, " during the first quarter of a century the inhabitants of the Northern States gradually sold their slaves to the South, where climate and the nature of the agricultural products increase the value of negro labour," all of which sounds as if the countryman of Von Holst had drawn his inspiration from the pro-slavery pamphlets of Buchanan's Administration.'

" I have not seen this letter, nor do I know who is the

writer, but if you will allow me space I think I can convince even the *Nation*, and its readers who shall happen to see this communication, that the statements quoted are not so wide of the mark as the *Nation* seems to think.

" If such, as the *Nation* suggests, was indeed the source of the writer's information, can the following facts and figures, which are taken mostly from a work of that time, be disputed? The author from whom I take the figures, as I cannot at this moment put my hand upon the census of 1790, was, it is true, a Rebel brigadier, the heroic defender of Marye's Heights at Fredericksburg, where he was killed; but, all the same, can the statements be denied?—(' Cobb on Slavery,' Philadelphia, T. and I. W. Johnson and Co., 1858) :—

" By the census of 1790 there were 40,370 slaves in the States north of Virginia. Now how were those 40,000 slaves emancipated? Can any one point to a single Act by any Northern State by which any negro was actually and immediately emancipated? We ask this because it is clear that all the gradual emancipation schemes had just the effect which the Frankfort writer states : to wit, they caused the inhabitants of the Northern States generally to sell their slaves to the South. Laws prohibiting slavery after some future date were but warnings to the owners of slaves to send them out of the State before the Act should go into effect. The inevitable working of such Acts was to send the slaves South for sale.

" Vermont, we know, claims the honour of having been the first to exclude slavery. She claims that this was done by her Bill of Rights in 1777. But the census of 1790 shows seventeen slaves. Her Bill of Rights could not have done a very perfect work since it allowed seventeen slaves to remain in bonds thirteen years after its adoption. Slavery, which had been introduced into Massachusetts soon after its first settlement, was ' tolerated,' as Chief Justice Parsons gently expresses it, certainly until the adoption of the Constitution of 1780.

P

Nor, indeed, did the Constitution of 1780, by any express provision or declaration, prohibit slavery. But a very few days
ago a letter of Mr. Thomas Silloway, of Boston, appeared in
the Charleston *Sun*, giving instances of bills of sale and disposition by will of Indian and negro slaves in Massachusetts as
late as 1771. Dr. Oliver Wendell Holmes makes Old Sophy,
the nurse of Elsie Venner, the daughter of a slave mother. So
gradual was the decadence of slavery in Massachusetts that as
late as 1833 her Supreme Court could not say by what specific
Act the institution had been abolished. (Winchendon v.
Hatfield, 4 Mass. 123 ; Commonwealth v. Aves, 18 Pick, 209.)

"In Belknap's ' New Hampshire,' Vol. III., 280, published
in 1792, the matter is thus explained :—

" 'Slavery is not prohibited by any express law. Negroes
were never very numerous in New Hampshire. Some of
them purchased their freedom during the late war by serving
three years in the army. Others have been made free by the
justice and humanity of their masters. In Massachusetts they
are all accounted free by the first article in the Declaration of
Rights, " All men are born free and equal." In the Bill of
Rights of New Hampshire the first article is expressed in these
words : "All men are born equally free and independent ;"
which, in the opinion of most persons, will bear the same
construction. But others have deduced from it this inference,
that all who are born since the Constitution was made are
free ; and that those who were in slavery before remain there
still. For this reason, in the late census, the blacks in New
Hampshire are distinguished into free and slaves. It is not in
my power to apologise for this inconsistency.'

" The author then goes on to explain, as we Southerners
afterwards continued to do, how much better off those who
were slaves were than those who were free in other States.
By the census of 1790 there were 158 slaves in New
Hampshire, and in 1840 there was still one remaining.

" In the plantations of Rhode Island slaves were more numerous than in the other New England States, as, indeed they necessarily were, considering that the merchants and sailors of that little State were the greatest slave traders of this country. But as the negroes could not thrive in that latitude, her Legislature provided a gradual scheme of emancipation, which took a lifetime to work out, leaving as late as 1840 five slaves in that State. Connecticut was too much interested to indulge her philanthropy at the expense of an immediate emancipation. In 1790 she had 2,750 slaves. So she too adopted a plan of gradual emancipation, by the slow and prudent workings of which seventeen of her slaves remained as such in 1840.

" As Mr. Bancroft observes : ' that New York is not a slave State like Carolina, is due to her climate and not to the superior humanity of her founders.' (Vol. II., 303). When South Carolina prohibited the importation of slaves from Africa in 1789, New York imported them and shipped the savages to this State as American slaves. As late as 1858 the London *Times* charged that New York had become the greatest slave-trading mart in the world, a charge which Wilson, in the ' Rise and Fall of the Slave Power,' fully corroborates. In 1790 New York had 21,324 slaves. She, too, adopted an Act of gradual emancipation, by the operation of which in 1840 all but four slaves had been gotten rid of. New Jersey, though adopting the same scheme, was slower in getting rid of her slaves, 674 still remaining in 1840.

" Adam Smith observed :—' The late resolution of the Quakers in Pennsylvania to set at liberty all their negro slaves may satisfy us that their number cannot be very great. Had they made any considerable part of their property such a resolution could never have been taken.' ('Wealth of Nations.') There were 3,737 slaves in Pennsylvania in 1790, and, as Adam Smith predicted, she would not sacrifice so much property. So

P 2

she, too, provided for gradual emancipation. The census of
1840 showed sixty-five negroes still in slavery. In 1823 a
negro woman was put up on the auction block along with some
machinery, smith's tools, and one cow, and sold for debt by the
sheriff of Fayette County, in the State of Brotherly Love. They
were still discussing this case in the Supreme Court of Pennsylvania as late as 1837, but it was the inadequacy of the price
the poor wretch brought, and not the iniquity of the transaction,
about which they were contending. (Lynch v. Commonwealth,
6 Watts 495.)   It was the frosts and snows which put an end
to slavery at the North, not philanthropy.

    " It is familiar history that the slave trade by which slavery
was established in this country was carried on by Old England
and New England, and not by the South.   As Mr. Lecky
points out, the New England trade, just prior to the Revolution, consisted in sending her lumber out and bringing
slaves in.

    " Some time since in his notes, in this same paper, while
reviewing a work on ' Brazil and Slavery,' the editor of the
Nation wrote as follows :—

    " ' We can recommend it for its own sake, but we have read
it with the deepest interest for its reflected light on that
irrepressible conflict which ended, some would say, in April,
1865, and others in March, 1876. First, and above all, it inspires
a sense of profound thankfulness that there never existed in this
country a party, or a policy, or a measure of gradual emancipation. We mean, of course, against that purely Southern slave
power which dictated the compromises of the Federal Constitution.'

    " In this the editor of the Nation could not have meant
that there never existed in this country a policy or a measure
of gradual emancipation, for, as we have seen, just such a
policy was adopted throughout the Northern States. It was
by just such measures that the Northern people rid themselves

of the institutions which they had so large a hand in imposing upon the South. But was this statement correct even if limited by his last sentence, ' We mean, of course, against the Southern slave power,' &c. ?

" Mr. Lincoln declared, in his inaugural address, that the Republican party had no intention to interfere with the institution of slavery; and Congress, by a joint resolution, approved July 22nd, 1861, repeated Mr. Lincoln's declaration, and announced to the South that the war was only for the preservation of the Union, and not for the abolition of slavery ; and Congress actually passed in March, 1861, by a two-thirds vote, a proposed amendment to the Constitution that :—

" ' No amendment shall be made to the Constitution which will authorise or give Congress the power to abolish or interfere within any State with the domestic institutions thereof, including that of persons held to labour or service by the laws of the said State.'

" Upon the recommendation, however, of Mr. Lincoln, made in a special message in April, 1862, Congress passed another joint resolution offering pecuniary aid from the General Government to induce the States to adopt 'general abolishment of slavery.'

" Mr. Lincoln expressed the sentiment of the North, which enabled him to carry on the war successfully, when, on the 22nd August, 1862, he said :

" ' My paramount object is to save the Union, and not to save or destroy slavery. If I could save the Union without freeing any slave I would do it. If I could save it by freeing all the slaves I would do it; and if I could do it by freeing some and leaving others alone, I would also do that.'

" The slaves in the States at war with the Federal Government were freed as a military and not as a political measure.

The Federal Government did not free the slaves in Delaware, Maryland, and Kentucky. The results of the war rendered slavery impracticable, but that was all.

"The truth is that the South could at any time during the war have secured the institution of slavery at the sacrifice of the right of secession. That sacrifice she would not voluntarily make, and she lost both her sovereignty and her slaves. She was the unfortunate, innocent, last holder of a dishonoured bill, and the emitters of it turned upon her and called to the world to see how they would punish her for holding it.

"EDWARD McCRADY, JR."

To this it may be added that, under the old territorial laws of Illinois, persons were allowed to bring slaves into the Territory under the name of indentured servants. As such they might be held in bondage for a term of ninety-nine years or less. This was in direct violation of the spirit of the ordinance of 1787, which interdicted slavery or involuntary servitude in all the territory north of the Ohio River. The first Illinois State Constitution, adopted in 1818, prohibited the further introduction of slaves, but did not abolish this species of slavery by liberating the victims of the old Territorial enactments. Thus slavery existed in Illinois in defiance of the ordinance of 1787 until the adoption of the Constitution of 1848, which contained the following provision :—"There shall be neither slavery nor involuntary servitude in this State, except as a punishment for crime." After the adoption of the Constitution of 1818, the first Legislature re-enacted the law "respecting free negroes, mulattoes, servants, and slaves" of Territorial times. No severer law was to be found in any slave State. It forbade negroes or mulattoes to settle in the State without certificates of freedom. No person was to employ any negro or mulatto without such certificate, under a penalty of $1.50 for each day. To harbour any slave or servant, or hinder the owner in retaking a slave, was made a felony, punishable by restitution or a fine of two-fold value, and by a whipping not to exceed thirty stripes. Every black or mulatto without a proper certificate was subject to arrest as a runaway slave, to be advertised for six weeks by the sheriff, when, if not reclaimed or his freedom established, he was sold for one year, after which he was entitled to a freedom certificate. Any slave or servant found ten miles from home without permit was liable to arrest and thirty-five stripes, on the order of a justice. For misbehaving to his master or family he was punishable with the lash. Indeed, punishment with the lash to the number of thirty-nine and forty stripes was prescribed for each of a long list of offences, real or of legal construction. Even after the adoption of the Constitution of 1848, which required the General Assembly at its first session to pass such laws as should effectually prohibit free persons of colour from immigrating to, or settling in this State, and should prohibit the owners of slaves from bringing them there for the purpose of setting them free, the Legislature passed an Act, February 12th, 1853, which imposed on every such coloured person a fine of $50. If the fine was not paid forthwith he was to be advertised and sold to any one who would pay the fine and costs for the shortest period of such person's service. A case under this law was carried up to the Supreme Court, and decided, so late as 1864, to be valid. Other provisions of these enactments, which were known as the Black Laws, were almost equally detestable. On February 7th, 1865, they were repealed. Had it not been for these Black Laws the census of Illinois would not be blotted with an enrolment of " 168 slaves " in 1810 ; 917 in 1820 ; 747 in 1830 ; and 331 in 1840—the last census that carries such a stain. Fortunately, the masters and people at large were better than their laws.

D.—THE GROWTH OF THE COLOURED RACE.

The following table shows the white and coloured populations of the whole of the United States at the various decennial perio ls from 1790 to the present time : —

Year.	Total White.	Coloured.	
		Free.	Slaves.
1790	3,172,006	59,527	697,681
1800	4,306,446	108,437	893,602
1810	5,862,073	186,446	1,191,362
1820	7,862,166	233,634	1,538,022
1830	10,537,378	319,599	2,009,043
1840	14,195,805	386,293	2,487,355
1850	19,553,068	434,495	3,204,313
1860	26,922,537	488,070	3,953,760
1870	33,589,377	4,880,009	none
1880	43,402,970	6,580,793	none
1890			none

INDEX.

———✧———

PRINTED BY CASSELL & COMPANY, LIMITED, LA BELLE SAUVAGE, LONDON, E.C.

www.ingramcontent.com/pod-product-compliance
Lightning Source LLC
Chambersburg PA
CBHW020851270326
41928CB00006B/653